GLOBAL CONNECTIONS

TERRORISM AND SECURITY

GLOBAL CONNECTIONS

America's Role in a Changing World
Changing Climates
The Changing Global Economy
Environment and Natural Resources
Feeding a Hungry World
The Human Population
Human Rights
One World or Many?
Pandemics and Global Health
Terrorism and Security

GLOBAL CONNECTIONS

TERRORISM AND SECURITY

ZORAN PAVLOVIĆ

SERIES EDITOR: CHARLES F. GRITZNER

CHELSEA HOUSE PUBLISHERS

An imprint of Infobase Publishing

Terrorism and Security

Chelsea House
An imprint of Infobase Publishing
132 West 31st Street
New York, NY 10001

Library of Congress Cataloging-in-Publication Data
Pavlovic, Zoran.
Terrorism and security / by Zoran Pavlovic.
p. cm. — (Global connections)
Includes bibliographical references and index.
ISBN 978-1-60413-282-3 (hardcover)
1. Terrorism—Juvenile literature. 2. National security—Juvenile literature. I. Title. II. Series.
HV6431.P388 2009
363.325—dc22 2008054883

Chelsea House books are available at special discounts when purchased in bulk quantities for businesses, associations, institutions, or sales promotions. Please call our Special Sales Department in New York at (212) 967-8800 or (800) 322-8755.

You can find Chelsea House on the World Wide Web at http://www.chelseahouse.com

Text design by Annie O'Donnell
Cover design by Takeshi Takahashi
Composition by EJB Publishing Service
Cover printed by IBT Global, Inc., Troy, NY
Book printed and bound by IBT Global, Inc., Troy, NY
Date printed: March 2011
Printed in the United States of America

10 9 8 7 6 5 4 3 2

This book is printed on acid-free paper.

All links and Web addresses were checked and verified to be correct at the time of publication. Because of the dynamic nature of the Web, some addresses and links may have changed since publication and may no longer be valid.

CONTENTS

INTRODUCTION

A GLOBAL COMMUNITY

Globalization is the process of coming together as a closely connected global community. It began thousands of years ago, when tribal groups and small hunting parties wandered from place to place. The process accelerated following Columbus's epic voyage more than five centuries ago. Europeans—an estimated 50 million of them—spread out to occupy lands throughout the world. This migration transformed the distribution of the world's peoples and their cultures forever. In the United States and Canada, for example, most people speak a West European language. Most practice a religious faith with roots in the ancient Middle East and eat foods originating in Asia.

Today, we are citizens of a closely interwoven global community. Events occurring half a world away can be watched and experienced, often as they happen, in our own homes. People, materials, and even diseases can be transported from continent to continent in a single day, thanks to jet planes. Electronic communications make possible the instantaneous exchange of information by phone, e-mail, or other means with friends or business associates almost anywhere in the world. Trade and commerce, perhaps more so than any other aspect of our daily lives, amply illustrate the importance of global linkages. How many things in your home (including your clothing) are of international origin? What foods and beverages have you consumed today that came from other lands? Could Northern America's economy survive without foreign oil, iron ore, copper, or other vital resources?

The GLOBAL CONNECTIONS series is designed to help you realize how closely people and places are tied to one another within the expanding global community. Each book introduces you to political, economic, environmental, social, medical, and other timely issues, problems, and prospects. The authors and editors hope you enjoy and learn from these books. May they hand you a passport to intellectual travels throughout our fascinating, complex, and increasingly "intradependent" world!

—Charles F. Gritzner
Series Editor

1

INTRODUCTION TO TERRORISM

With a barrage of gunfire followed by the explosion of a hand grenade, a group of a half dozen terrorists burst into the meeting room of Organization of Petroleum Exporting Countries (OPEC) ministers in Vienna, Austria. The group's leader was one of the world's most notorious terrorists. Ilich Ramirez Sanchez, better known as "Carlos the Jackal," worked closely with the Palestinian terrorists. Some of the ministers were executed on the spot, while others were taken hostage. Not long after, the terrorists and 42 hostages were on board a DC-9 flying to a terrorist-friendly (although unknown) destination in the Middle East or North Africa. The world was watching in disbelief. The year was 1975 and terrorism was breaking out across the globe.

Since the beginning of time, people have fought against one another. And, sadly, they will continue to fight. Survival is the most fundamental drive of all life-forms. In this regard, humans are no different than other species. Humans, like other social animals, belong to groups for protection in an attempt to ensure their survival. Archaeological evidence shows that during early human history, small units united by blood ties formed to protect one another. Such bands may represent the oldest social system still in existence.

Imagine groups of hunters and gatherers roaming the savannas of Africa together. They were more successful in providing food and shelter for one another than they would have been as individuals working alone. Fierce predators found it more difficult to snatch a human meal within a strong and cohesive social group. Because of the protection they offered, tiny bands continued to grow numerically and gradually absorb others. Yet in order to enjoy the newly found shelter, the latest to arrive had to sacrifice their previously held independence.

Newcomers were smaller in number, and their power within their adopted band was minimal. Under the circumstances, however, they had no options if they were to benefit from protection against outsiders. A social system of leaders and followers, haves and have nots, gradually emerged as one result of this social arrangement. The sense of belonging to each level of the new social environment was formed on the basis of common ancestry. Members of a larger group would install their own relatives as leaders. Newcomers found that they had little if any influence over the band's important decisions. Such conditions gradually led to sharp divisions and growing dissent among members of the subdued, or minority, group. In order to improve their status, they revolted, often violently.

Retaliation for such action was quick and harsh. In the end, the stronger and dominant group within the band emerged as the winner in the conflict. Those unwilling to commit to the group were killed, punished in some other way, or expelled to find refuge elsewhere. Ravage and fear as methods of control, violent revolt, and harsh retaliation are ancient concepts, as the foregoing example illustrates. Today we call these practices *terrorism*.

TERRORISTS AND FREEDOM FIGHTERS

There is an expression that states, "What to one person is terrorism, is a brave and patriotic act of freedom to another." For this reason and others, it is extremely difficult to define terrorism. Terrorism, itself, is not a goal. Rather, it is a method by which various individuals and groups attempt to achieve certain goals. Nearly all terrorist acts are undertaken to achieve some goal, as bizarre as the objective may appear to others. Those who apply terrorism as a means of achieving goals often believe that they are on a mission. They believe themselves to be freedom fighters, or liberators, in pursuit of justice for themselves or their cause.

In many instances, terrorism is seen as being the only available option when political dialogue fails. A thin line, however, separates terrorists from freedom fighters. How we use these labels often depends on who wins the battle or war. Winners, after all, write history books, and winners are not inclined to be critical of their own actions!

Surprisingly, perhaps, terrorism has a long history in the United States. Acts of terrorism, sometimes incredibly brutal, are found throughout the nation's cultural history. To this day, residents of eastern Kansas, for example, remember stories about the Civil War's atrocities that occurred in the area. In 1863, a large group of pro-South and proslavery guerrilla raiders attacked the city of Lawrence after crossing from Missouri. Lawrence's residents at that time supported the Union and advocated the abolition of slavery. Led by one of the most infamous characters of the Civil War era, William Quantrill, the raiders savagely ravaged the small town. Scores of civilian residents lost their lives in execution-style murders.

Many of those killed had nothing to do with the active participation in the war, but Quantrill's troops showed no mercy. Their goal was to show the people of Kansas that there was a price to pay for supporting abolitionism and the North. The rest of pro-Union Kansas received this powerful message of fear loud and clear.

In Missouri, on the other hand, those who participated in the attack on Lawrence gained folk-hero status within proslavery circles. Soon after the massacre in Lawrence, Jayhawkers and Union troops crossed the Missouri border. (Jayhawkers were Kansas pro-Union guerrillas similar to Quantrill's raiders in their methods.) Determined that civilians in Missouri pay an equally heavy price, the Jayhawkers retaliated with vengeance. Although both sides committed terrible atrocities, the Union won the Civil War. In so doing, it also won the right to interpret history favoring the militias who fired rounds from Union-supplied firearms. Therefore, Jayhawkers are remembered as freedom fighters, while Quantrill's raiders are considered terrorists.

ORIGINS OF MODERN TERRORISM

The term *terrorism* appears frequently in regard to events following the French Revolution of 1789. After the monarchy's collapse, the country was in a state of disarray. Various factions sought political power. Public executions left thousands dead. Terror was rampant among the ordinary French who lived in constant fear of losing their heads to the guillotine. The period of chaos became known as the Reign of Terror. Since then, the terms *terror* and *terrorism* identify violent actions against the community that occur for ideological reasons. Such actions rarely acknowledge the universal moral obligation to prevent the loss of civilian lives during combat.

Recognizing someone as a true terrorist creates a difficult dilemma. The subject of terrorism falls under a vast gray area of interpretation; it does not lend itself to a simple black-and-white definition. The issue is complicated by the concept of morality. While the foundations for many national constitutions are moral values, laws are not interpreted on the basis of morality. Many organizations recognized by world bodies as terrorist groups

Contrary to popular belief, terrorism has a long history in the United States. This 1863 illustration from *Harper's Weekly* shows William Quantrill and his rebel troops killing the citizens of Lawrence, Kansas, and setting the town's buildings on fire. This terrorist act was carried out in the name of defending slavery.

actually avoid purposely hurting civilians. They do so for political appeal, that is, to receive public, political, and financial support. In such instances, they aim toward the destruction of property and harm to security forces, police, and military personnel.

Northern Ireland's long-lasting conflict between Roman Catholics and Protestants serves as a good example. By avoiding civilian deaths, some factions of the Irish Republican Army (IRA)—the group associated with Roman Catholic interests and those of the Irish Republic—wanted to be known as freedom fighters. They wanted to appeal to the local supporters but also tried to influence positive feelings from the international public. IRA factions willing to compromise received public support.

Previously labeled as terrorists, many are now public figures and politicians. IRA factions that continued to use civilian targets in their attacks were, however, harshly condemned by many of their own supporters. Eventually, they lost their credibility and, along with it, much of their support base.

GLOBAL CONNECTIONS

The twentieth century witnessed a rapid expansion of terrorism on all inhabited continents. Wars for independence in Africa, Eurasia, and Latin America served as training grounds for terrorists and the growth of terrorism. The Cold War (mid-1940s to early 1990s) set up a global theater in which ideological differences frequently were discussed through the barrel of a gun or by the sickening blast of a car bomb. Two superpowers—the United States and the Soviet Union (USSR)—both worked closely with organizations responsible for terrorism. These countries justified their actions by believing that the end justifies the means. The Soviet Union provided much assistance to Socialist and Communist revolutionaries known for their brutality. The United States supported many regimes and guerrilla groups. They ranged from democratic to outright totalitarian and ultra-right-wing, particularly in Latin America and portions of Asia.

As global technology and communication have expanded, the public awareness of terrorist organizations and acts has grown accordingly. Conventionally fought wars are but a distant memory to many citizens. On the other hand, nearly everyone is aware of terrorism and the threat of terrorists. News of events that used to be reported only locally can now spread worldwide almost instantaneously. Contemporary terrorists and their backers have learned that the highest possible public exposure can come with a minimal cost. A car bombing in Spain, an elementary school invasion in the Caucasus region, or an assassination in Pakistan are immediately reported through electronic and print media.

In the years following the end of the Cold War, much of the developing world went through a period of radical geopolitical (political geography) change. The balance of political power between the United States and the USSR shifted in favor of the United States. Economic globalization introduced social and

MAKING CONNECTIONS

TERRORISTS OR FREEDOM FIGHTERS?

Nigeria, Africa's most diverse and populous country, is blessed with mineral wealth. Its vast petroleum reserves contribute billions of dollars in oil revenues annually. At the same time, Nigeria's public officials are among the world's most corrupt. Oil profits are mismanaged, funds are stolen, and the country and most of its people remain poor. Energy-producing areas in the Niger River delta receive little in economic help (compared to their contribution to Nigeria's income) and poverty is rampant. These factors contribute to growing ethnic tensions.

Residents of the oil-producing delta region demanded a redistribution of oil revenues. They also wanted major improvements in protecting the environment and in the region's miserable living conditions. When their requests went unanswered, the violence began. Armed groups of delta residents began to destroy pipelines and other facilities. They even attacked workers on oil rig platforms. These "terrorists" consider themselves to be fighters for what is right. They want some of the oil riches taken from their land to be used locally, to help improve their own living standards. They want the terrible destruction of their natural environment to cease. They want to be freed from oppression. And they want to see an end to the terrible corruption that is holding their country back. But many Nigerians, including the country's government, see them as terrorists who must be stopped. In this "terrorist" conflict, who do you believe is morally and legally correct?

political reforms to a previously unimagined extent. Not everyone, however, embraced the new age. This is particularly true of those who felt that these changes posed a threat to their long-standing cultural values. These conditions contributed to the development of the first major international terrorist organization, al Qaeda. It redefined terrorism from a local to a global force of destruction. In the past, few terrorist organizations aspired to operate beyond national or regional boundaries. They may have acquired inspiration and initial knowledge from similar movements elsewhere. Their basic operations and logistics, however, were geographically limited. Not even the calls for a global Communist revolution managed to create a similar movement.

Even the network that has a global reach, al Qaeda, relies on a simple explanation to justify its deadly actions. They explain terrorism as a matter of survival against the invasion of their culture (way of life) and their sacred Islamic land (Saudi Arabia). They believe that those who hold power in the world (the United States and the West) are responsible for most of the world's troubles. As a result, it is their obligation to fight against "evil" in what has been labeled a *jihad*, or "holy war."

The simplicity of this approach helps attract a significant number of followers from diverse backgrounds. They all seem to have a common goal, which is to increase their power. In regard to terrorism, few things have really changed since ancient times. People continue to fight with one another because their goals remain the same. It is only the methods used to fight that have changed over time.

This book provides insights on the evolution of modern terrorism and describes its effects on global society. When, for example, did suicide bombing originate, and how is it practiced throughout the world? Why do only a limited number of terrorist organizations practice suicide bombings? How did European political ideas make their way to other regions where they were often used to fuel conflicts and terrorist activities? These and other important questions will be answered in the pages of this book.

2

A GLOBAL AGE OF TERRORISM

Today we live in an increasingly *intra*dependent global community in which no one can remain isolated. Actions occurring in one part of the globe can cause immediate reactions half a world away. Scarcely a day passes without news agencies and 24-hour cable network stations reporting some type of terrorist activity. It may seem that terror attacks have occurred more often in recent years. In fact, the frequency of terrorist activities has not risen drastically during recent decades. What is occurring is that terrorist activities are becoming more diverse. Terrorism also has hit much closer to home and with greater destruction than in times past.

Many terrorist acts occurred during the 1960s and 1970s. Most of them were associated with ethnic groups struggling for freedom or conflicts between groups with different political beliefs. Since then, terrorism has become more complex and more varied. Western countries, in particular, have fallen victim to this diversification. Environmental terrorism, for example, has become quite commonplace in the United States and elsewhere in the developed world. Opponents of genetically modified food frequently have resorted to force and destruction to send their message to the world. So have those opposed to the use of animals for such purposes as providing meat or pelts, or for laboratory testing. Their methods include the burning of crops, the destruction of research laboratories, and the harassment of those with whom they disagree. The debate over abortion policies also has led to violence. Abortion clinics have been bombed and a number of medical professionals have been killed. Latin American drug trafficking cartels, too, are experts in spreading fear through killings of ordinary citizens and assassinations of public officials.

Terrorism has many faces, a reality that has formed many changes in protection and security. Security agencies have had to develop new approaches in their attempts to stay a step ahead of terrorists. In the past, most nations relied on their own law-enforcing agencies to protect them from terrorism. Cooperation between or among countries and agencies generally was limited to pursuit of international fugitives or notorious common criminals. Even in the United States, different security agencies such as the Federal Bureau of Investigation (FBI), the Central Intelligence Agency (CIA), and local law enforcement agencies rarely exchanged information. The September 11, 2001, attacks ushered in a new age of counterterrorism security. The terrorists were international. And they had effectively used a network of international connections while planning their deadly attacks. They also successfully avoided authorities in several countries, further adding to the international dimension of their scheme.

Today, global terrorism faces global security. Law enforcement bodies in North America, Europe, and elsewhere cooperate in creating terrorism-related databases. They continuously exchange the latest information about potential terrorist threats. Ingenious methods and flexibility are what terrorism thrives on. Therefore, security agencies must constantly create new and more sophisticated methods of protection.

CULTURE CHANGE AND TERRORISM

Historically, at one point all people in the world lived in a rural cultural environment. They practiced folk culture, or a very traditional way of life. Some hunted, fished, and gathered for their livelihood. Others farmed or herded livestock as their primary economic activity. Communities formed through direct family ties or tribal connections. Only occasionally did they venture far from the local area. Close personal ties and a very slow pace of change were the hallmarks of such a society. Age-old tribal rules served as the primary and unwritten laws by which people lived. Everyone knew the rules and how to follow them.

Each new generation was born into a cultural environment that had changed very little from that of their ancestors. One could not prosper without his or her community's support. Social and geographical isolation protected them against outside influences. The core of a folk group's identity—its cultural and social values—remained little changed over the centuries.

Then the world around these traditional societies began to change. In a matter of decades—first in Western Europe and then in other regions—industrialization and urbanization brought development and rapid "progress." Cities began to sprout up around factories. People held jobs for which they received wages, ushering in a cash economy. Traditional country people had to have an intimate understanding of their natural surroundings in order to survive. City folk had to be formally educated and able to read, write, and work with numbers in order to compete successfully in a fast-paced urban society. People demanded both individual liberties and laws to protect them. For the first time in recorded history, gender equality turned into a prospective reality. Previously, women had few options. Their lives in a male-dominated society revolved around childbearing and household work. Society's focus began to be on the individual rather than on the group. This shift was a tremendous cultural change that challenged many existing beliefs, attitudes, and practices.

Many people, particularly males, saw these changes not as an improvement, but as the threatening loss of an age-old cultural system. They feared that cultural values—the very essence of their lifestyle and identity—were going to vanish. What once had been a majority (the band, tribe, or some other tightly knit group) suddenly became the minority. Modern national constitutions soon replaced unwritten traditional laws. Village elders lost their status within the community. Many men felt a loss of power as women rose in social status and influence. Wealth and social position were no longer based upon hunting, farming, herding, or other traditional skills. Success in the new culture and society was based upon education and professional specialization. Former leaders suddenly found themselves in the position of follower.

Under such circumstances, many people became frustrated and increasingly desperate. No one, it seemed, cared about them or their needs in the new urban society. In order to preserve their identity and status, some saw violence as the only way out of their dilemma. They fought to preserve their cultural values and personal honor, as well as the survival of traditions their ancestors had practiced for thousands of years. Accepting anything but a return to the past system was seen as defeat. These are the cultural conditions in which terrorism and terrorists thrive.

The developing world is currently undergoing the process described in the foregoing scenario. It is one that will continue for quite some time—generations, in fact. Various countries are in different stages of transition. Not surprisingly, we see the spread of violent culture wars, ethnic struggles, and religious conflicts mainly in developing countries. Tribal areas of Afghanistan and Pakistan's western frontier, the Caucasus region in the former Soviet Union, and southeast Europe serve as excellent examples of cultural transition. They are also the regional hotbeds of terrorist activity. Latin American Indians have engaged in guerrilla warfare and terrorism numerous times in order to preserve their own way of life.

Terrorism in response to this type of cultural transition is enormously difficult to prevent or control. Most such activities have strong popular support in the areas where terrorists operate. New recruits arrive from local villages and are given food and shelter by local farmers. Security deficiencies in Afghanistan, for example, are directly related to cooperation between villagers and terrorists. In a folk culture setting, it is an honor (and a responsibility) to help one's neighbor, even if he or she is a terrorist.

POLITICAL AND IDEOLOGICAL DIFFERENCES

Political parties and movements often count on terrorism as a means of solving ideological differences. In the democratic political system, terrorist actions are rare because democracies encourage political participation and freedom of expression. Much of the world, however, is still composed of only partially democratic or entirely totalitarian (ruled by a dictatorial government) nations. In such circumstances, a political party may rise to prominence by illegally overthrowing the elected government and establishing a dictatorship. Once the new government comes to power, it immediately takes action to silence all those who oppose it.

The next step for the new government is to rewrite the constitution and to establish a political system that at least on the surface appears to be open and democratic. In reality, the new constitution often supports the new system that does not allow active opposition. Sooner or later, the political turnover leads to violence. In many countries, this approach has led to serious unrest and even civil wars.

In the early 1990s, Algeria fell into deadly internal turmoil that lasted for several years. During this period, nearly a quarter million Algerians became victims of terrorism-related killings. Conflict began after the pro-Islamic party, the Islamic Salvation Front (FIS), won the first round of the national elections. Before the next round of balloting could begin, the country's military intervened, seized power, and abolished the electoral process. In so doing, it effectively banned the party that won the first round of voting. Members of FIS began guerrilla warfare, including targeting civilians. The "government" acted similarly against anyone who it believed supported FIS. Car bombs, assassinations, and even executions of foreign workers occurred on a regular basis. Although the conflict officially ended by 2002, occasional bombings and killings still contribute to news headlines in the troubled country.

The 1960s were a troubled period. Many left-wing guerrilla groups supported a Communist revolution and dictatorship over the working class. Revolutions continued through the 1970s and 1980s, although with less intensity. In 1991, the Soviet Union was dissolved and the Cold War abruptly ended. Many left-wing movements disbanded. Others became integrated into the democratic process in their countries. Groups inspired by ideology operate in many countries. Nepal's Marxist guerrillas, for example, terrorized the countryside and continued to fight security forces until 2007. Their goal was to overthrow the now-abolished monarchy. In Colombia, revolutionaries hide away in the dense tropical rain forests and launch attacks, assassinations, and kidnappings.

Religious fundamentalism is becoming an increasingly important factor in regard to global terrorism. Terrorist organizations are well aware of the powerful status religion holds in the lives of the ordinary people. They are able to use people's devout faith for their own benefit. There are many instances in which people supported terrorists solely because the group pledged to fight for their religion. Using religion is another skillful way of acquiring public support. For example, the people of Lebanon share all aspects of lifestyle except religion. The country is deeply divided along religious lines and has suffered greatly from terrorist activities. That sole cultural trait—religion—was enough to keep the country in civil turmoil for several decades. Christians and Muslims quickly separated and chose their sides once the fighting began. Similarly, most Iraqis are of Arab ethnic origin.

Yet the slight variation in Islamic tradition is enough to separate Sunni from Shia, resulting in bloody violence among members of the respective sects.

ETHNIC CONFLICTS

It is very difficult for most minority ethnic groups to be fully accepted by a country's major ethnicity. As a result, many minorities suffer "second class" (or worse) citizenship. In this situation, it is easy for warmongers in the ethnic minority to use violence in order to achieve their goals. Often, they are pursuing independent status for their group. Because ethnic militias do not have much military power (unless it is supplied by an outside source), they often rely on terrorism and/or guerrilla-type attacks to make an impact.

Two examples of ethnic conflicts and terrorism are the Kurds in Southwest Asia (parts of Iran, Iraq, Syria, and Turkey) and the Basques in Spain. Both groups are fighting for full independence within their respective regions. Neither rebellion can be branded as a "religious conflict," because in both instances religion is not a dividing factor. Kurds, like the Turks, are Muslim; Basques, like most Spaniards, are Roman Catholic.

Although they are one of the oldest ethnic groups in the region, the Kurds have never been able to establish their own nation-state. They are scattered throughout Southwest Asia, but the majority reside inside Turkey's boundaries. Other than claiming a different ethnic heritage and language, Kurds differ little from Turks. Yet both sides believe their differences are great enough for the Kurds to want a separate state and for Turkey's government to ban usage of the Kurdish language. Several Kurdish factions regularly attack Turkey's military which, in turn, responds with drastic retaliation.

Basques are of the same religious faith as their neighbors, but they speak a different language and are ethnically unrelated to anyone in the region. Their roots trace back to the earliest people

Differences in religion and ideology lead some terrorists to attack places of worship. *Above*, parts of a mosque north of Baghdad are reduced to rubble after a 2006 terrorist attack. The explosion led to fierce sectarian fighting between Sunnis and Shiites across Iraq.

who inhabited the Iberian Peninsula (Spain and Portugal) before the arrival of Spain's other peoples. During Francisco Franco's rule (1939–1973) any display of nationalism other than Spanish was immediately suppressed. The inability to "be themselves" and enjoy their own ethnic uniqueness further infuriated the Basques. It strengthened their resistance and provided additional fuel for their drive toward nationalism and independence. Since the early 1960s, Basque terrorists have claimed responsibility for hundreds of military and civilian deaths. The Basque terrorist organization is Euskadi Ta Askatasuna (ETA). It formed in 1959 in response to the extreme pressure being put on Basques by Spain's then Fascistic (extreme right-wing dictatorship) regime.

The ETA engages in terrorist acts such as car bombings, assassinations, and kidnappings to pursue the Basque goal of forming a country independent from Spain.

STATE-SPONSORED TERRORISM

Some governments openly support groups labeled as terrorist organizations by the United Nations and other international bodies. Others secretly provide such assistance as funding, military supplies, and sanctuary havens for wanted terrorists. This is where the line dividing freedom fighting and terrorism enters uncharted waters. It all depends on one's perceptions and interpretations. It also depends on the international status and power of a country accused of sponsoring terrorists.

Democratic countries have funded opposition groups with terrorist ties with the goal of destabilizing other countries. There are several stages of support in such circumstances. The first stage is silent approval. A country simply looks in a different direction when atrocities are committed. Then, when it becomes impossible to ignore the situation any longer, public officials announce that in a struggle for freedom the ends sometimes justify the means. It is important for them to justify their violent methods in deposing unpopular regimes. Terrorism, after all, stands against everything democratic nations believe in. This is hypocrisy, but it must appear as a morally just act to support freedom.

When terrorist acts are committed, most are explained away as isolated incidents by individuals, rather than as acts of antigovernment forces or other organized groups. Negative public opinion, however, may continue. If this occurs, stronger steps may be taken, including full-fledged assistance and even military intervention to depose the existing government. This may take place without international consensus or support. Moral values seem to vanish in this context. Economic and political interests hold much greater importance in making these kinds of decisions.

One example of this is the Cuban Revolution. In 1959, revolutionaries led by Fidel Castro overthrew Fulgencio Batista's dictatorship. Batista fled to Miami, Florida, and Castro ascended to power. It soon became clear that Castro's policies were far from democratic. His government took control of private property and foreign investments. He expanded diplomatic and military ties with the Soviet Union. American economic and political interests in Cuba became increasingly endangered. Giant corporations like United Fruit were in fear of losing huge profits. The U.S. government became deeply concerned that other Castro-like revolutionaries would attempt to take over other Latin American countries. Stopping the spread of left-wing ideas and governments in Central and South America became a top U.S. foreign policy priority.

The United States broke its diplomatic relationship with the Castro government and began a program to overthrow the new regime. The program included channeling funds to anti-Castro Cubans and overseeing covert operations, including assassinations. Camps on American soil served as training centers for Cuban "freedom fighters." In the spring of 1961, the CIA masterminded an invasion of Cuba by these freedom fighters. Despite careful planning, the invasion—which came to be known as the Bay of Pigs—was a total fiasco. About 1,400 of the anti-Castro Cubans who landed on Cuba's southern shore either were killed or taken prisoner. Fidel Castro survived the close call. In addition to the ill-fated invasion, Fidel Castro claims to have survived hundreds of assassination attempts. Nonetheless, in power for nearly a half century, Castro was one of the longest-ruling strongmen of recent times. The Bay of Pigs invasion was a tremendous blow to the White House and to President John F. Kennedy. Despite America's claim to being a "champion of democracy," the entire world knew that it was the United States that had funded the clandestine operation.

Another example occurred in Chile. In 1973, three years after being democratically elected the president of Chile, Salvador

Allende was dead. His Socialist policies—primarily nationalization of many financial and industrial interests—directly conflicted with American interests in the Chilean economy. Allende additionally aggravated the U.S. government by establishing closer ties with the Communist governments of the Soviet Union, Cuba, and the People's Republic of China. Of major U.S. concern was the Chilean government's attempt to seize American corporations' lucrative copper mines. There was a growing fear that Allende would become another Castro. The White House was particularly concerned over the loss of American-owned property in Chile. It feared that such a takeover in one country would encourage other governments to do the same. Of particular concern were economic interests in oil-rich countries where American oil corporations had much at stake. At the time, Algeria, Libya, and Iraq already were nationalizing parts of the oil industry in their respective countries.

The CIA's support of anti-Allende groups resulted in nationwide strikes, the assassination of the highest-ranking military officers, and ultimately a coup d'état and Allende's death. Augusto Pinochet, the U.S.-backed general who was one of the coup's leaders, became president. He was the clear choice of the right-wing military junta that gained control of the country. During his time in office, civil liberties were widely trampled upon. Countless Chileans died under mysterious circumstances or simply vanished. Left-wing political opposition was banned entirely. Henry Kissinger, the former U.S. national security advisor, was actively involved in the Chilean affairs of the 1970s. Because of his role more than three decades ago, he must plan his vacation trips differently than most Americans. Kissinger consults his lawyers before international travel out of concern that he might be indicted by various foreign governments!

State-sponsored terrorism is often difficult to prove. Governments make every attempt to deny or cover up their involvement. They do this in the hope of avoiding international outrage over their actions. In 1988, a Boeing 747 exploded over the Scottish town of Lockerbie, killing all 259 people on board. Eleven local residents died as well when one fuel-carrying wing of the aircraft fell on their houses, creating an inferno. An investigation soon proved that someone planted a bomb in the plane's cargo section. An explosion caused the plane to separate into pieces that were widely scattered about the countryside. Most passengers were American citizens. This made the attack the most devastating in U.S. history up to that time.

A Libyan intelligence officer, Abdelbaset Ali Mohmed al-Megrahi, was singled out as the mastermind of the Lockerbie tragedy. But Libya denied any wrongdoing and refused to extradite its citizen. Eleven years passed before economic sanctions imposed by the United Nations nudged the Libyan leadership to finally change its mind. The government allowed al-Megrahi to face trial, and he was finally convicted for his heinous crime. Another suspect from Libya was prosecuted but was declared not guilty on all charges.

UNINTENDED CONSEQUENCES

Terrorism can result from poor decision-making by great powers. Their inability to understand the possible consequences of geopolitical decisions has given birth to many terrorist movements. Among the largest blunders of the modern era was the American carpet bombing of Cambodia during the Vietnam War. North Vietnamese forces infiltrated Cambodia and used it as a support base. In response, American bombers secretly (without the U.S. Congress's knowledge and approval) attacked Cambodia, leveling villages. Rather than increase the country's security, the bombing campaign destabilized Cambodia. It set in motion the chaotic conditions that eventually allowed the Cambodian Communists, the Khmer Rouge, to gain power. Their program of "reeducating masses" is now remembered as the Killing Fields, one of recent history's most horrible examples of genocide.

ECOTERRORISM

Compared to other forms of terrorism, which can be incredibly merciless, ecoterrorism is more a nuisance than a threat to society. In fact, some critics suggest that the term "terrorism" is inappropriately used in this context. Those labeled "ecoterrorists" insist that their intention is not to cause loss of human lives. They campaign against animal mistreatment and cruelty, as well as the destruction of the natural environment. Their goal is to increase the quality of life for society by generating public concern for various issues. Two organizations are particularly well known for their ecoterrorist activities: the Animal Liberation Front and the Earth Liberation Front. Both were formed in the United Kingdom and are particularly active in northern America.

Despite claims of "peacefulness," these and similar groups hold high status on the FBI's list of terrorist groups. FBI officials have stated that the groups have been responsible for destroying laboratories, arson, and the use of explosives. These are just some of the reasons they have earned the ecoterrorist label. In the United States alone, millions of dollars of property and research data are lost annually to ecoterrorist actions.

Ecoterrorists, surprisingly, often turn to deliberate destruction of the natural environment to pursue their goal of—environmental preservation! In an attempt to stop penetration of formerly pristine woodlands by developers, a protestor can light a single match that can destroy millions of dollars in property. In recent years, southern Europe and parts of the United States have suffered many devastating forest fires. Many were deliberately set. During summer months, areas that experience a Mediterranean climate (including highly developed Mediterranean Europe and Southern California) become tinder dry. Highly flammable grasses and dominant types of bushes, shrubs, and trees form most of the plant life within this climate and ecosystem. Summer rainfall is sparse, and temperatures are high. These conditions are ideal for the start and rapid spread of raging wildfires. Settlements and other elements of the landscape can be destroyed in moments and often result in enormous financial loss. Prevention of such acts is difficult, if not impossible.

ASSASSINATIONS AND KIDNAPPINGS

One of the oldest terrorist practices is murdering for the sake of destabilizing society and destroying its morale. Assassination of a public leader sends a message to the public. It shows that terrorists have an ability to strike at random wherever they want. If the assassinated leader was freely elected, the death is less apt to cause chaos. This is because in a democratic society, a person holding public office—even a prime minister or a president—is

On December 23, 1988, a bomb onboard Pan American Flight 103 caused the aircraft to explode over Lockerbie, Scotland. Eleven villagers and all on board were killed.

only one link in the chain that is the decision-making process. Nonetheless, public backlash against such assassins is always high. When ruthless autocratic leaders and dictators are assassinated, there is a chance for positive change to occur. When a despot is assassinated, there may be little, if any, public backlash against the terrorists.

The kidnapping and execution of an Italian prime minister, Aldo Moro, in 1978 caused a public backlash. One of Italy's leading political figures, Moro was kidnapped by the Communist terrorists known as the Red Brigades and was held hostage for almost two months. At the time of his kidnapping, Moro was attempting to strengthen cooperation between opposing political parties. He sought to form a more productive government by increasing interaction between Christian Democrats and Communists. During that period, the kidnappers demanded the release of imprisoned comrades in exchange for Moro. After negotiations failed, Moro's body was found, riddled with bullets, in the trunk of a car parked on a Rome street. Public opinion immediately turned against the terrorists, and they lost even the little support they had previously had.

High-profile assassinations can trigger a global response if conditions are ripe for conflict. An example is the 1914 killing of Austria's successor to the throne, Archduke Franz Ferdinand, in Sarajevo, Bosnia and Herzegovina. His assassination triggered the beginning of the First World War. Eventually, that terrible conflict directly or indirectly involved most of the world's countries, including the United States. Half a century later, the assassination of American president John F. Kennedy in Dallas, Texas, shocked not only the nation but the rest of the world. His death came only a year after the threat of the 1962 Cuban Missile Crisis and the accompanying threat of a nuclear war between the United States and the USSR. Many believe that Lee Harvey Oswald, supposedly acting alone, was the killer. Unfortunately, before a trial could be held, Oswald himself died at the hands of an assassin. Had an outside force, particularly one with Cuban or Soviet ties, been found to be responsible for Kennedy's death, the nuclear crisis could have easily reignited.

Today, more than ever before, local assassinations produce global implications. Escalation of Pakistan's political crisis led to the assassination of Benazir Bhutto in 2007. Bhutto was the country's former prime minister and the widely supported opposition leader. Her death from a suicide bombing occurred just before the scheduled national elections. The government accused terrorist group al Qaeda and its supporters of plotting the assassination. In this example, the violent death of a popular leader happened in a country with a stockpile of nuclear weapons. Pakistan also has a turbulent relationship with neighboring India and considerable instability among its own people. Conditions such as these are enough to cause deep concern in many national capitals and political forums.

ANTIGLOBALIZATION TERRORISM

In recent years, yet another form of terrorism began to receive considerable attention—antiglobalization terrorism. Despite overwhelming evidence that globalization is contributing to global economic development, some forces are unwilling to compromise on this issue. Proponents of economic globalization support free market capitalism. They face stern resistance from those who view capitalism as another form of imperialism and foreign oppression. Violent acts against globalization frequently occur in developed countries. The negative stance on globalization is directed against United States–based corporations. Protests are particularly vehement against those companies that are responsible for the spread of American popular culture.

Attacks on McDonald's restaurants in France illustrate the resistance to globalization. The French, who go to great lengths to protect their own cultural values, see McDonald's fast-food restaurants as a symbol of American cultural imperialism. The argument against McDonald's is that it infringes on the French way of life. They see mass-produced fast food as a threat to French cuisine and their tradition of long sit-down meals. Of course, it also poses a threat to segments of the French economy. Opponents argue that the giant faceless corporations soon will rule their daily social and cultural routines and will pose a threat to local, small-scale restaurants. Hamburgers were, in fact, invented in Europe. Yet, when billions and billions of pieces of ground beef are served by an American corporation, European perceptions tend to change!

In reality, the issue of McDonald's and other (American) corporations invading France and other countries has two essential aspects. First, ordinary people are generally unaware of how large corporation-based (macroeconomic) systems function as part of globalization. Their response is based on opinions that have little if any economic basis. Half-true statements such as "the Big Mac makes one fat" can be used as political tools to gain public support.

A second, and much more important, aspect of globalization is that ideally, capitalism should be free of government interference. In this context, "free" means without regulations and barriers. It allows private enterprise to flourish and, as is supported by historical evidence, stimulates the fastest economic development. Economic globalization and removal of barriers disrupt the control government has over a country's economy. In developed European countries, governments carefully oversee aspects of the economy. Sectors range from energy production to national airline carriers, roads and railroads, and even some agricultural production. Government control provides additional state revenue, which, in turn, funds social programs such as universal health care.

Agriculture provides a good example of government involvement. To support local farmers and crop production, governments set high tariffs (fees imposed upon imported goods) for foreign companies seeking to conduct business in their countries. This keeps the cost of local products artificially low. It also protects local production and workers, both of which could be threatened by a flood of cheaper imports. In reality, however, such protectionist policies are counterproductive. They tend to hinder long-term economic expansion because they hinder fair competition and also discourage foreign investments. If a country is to continue to grow economically, such protections must be removed to allow the free flow of goods and services.

When protections are removed, farmers feel threatened by economic competition. They, of course, blame globalization for their hardship. Their concerns are soon picked up by the general public. Eventually, attentions—and outrage—focus upon the perceived source of their problem: globalization.

Attacks against globalization take many forms. Some protestors lash out verbally, while others riot. McDonald's workers have to clean vandalized restaurants or face the loss of their jobs when restaurants are destroyed by fire. In fear for their own prosperity, desperate people use desperate measures. Today, American establishments are attacked. Tomorrow, perhaps, Chinese, British, or Brazilian businesses will receive similar treatment.

Such attacks still represent a minor issue compared to other terrorism-related activities. As the world progresses into the next economic era, we may certainly expect to experience more antiglobalization sentiment and terrorism. The developing world is where terrorism with antiglobalization undertones is on a rapid rise. The governments there, particularly nonelected regimes, systematically play the antiglobalization card as a tool for controlling basic freedoms of their people.

In North Korea, the ruling elite oversee the economy, as well as nearly all other aspects of life. Printed and electronic media, personal possessions, and leisure travel are strictly regulated in order for the Communist government to remain locked in power. Those who fail to follow government-imposed rules are imprisoned or even executed. The entire nation is under constant fear of what will happen next. At the same time, North Korea's unwillingness to open itself up to the world's economic system has brought the

Antiglobalization activists demonstrate outside a Paris McDonald's in 2003. Terrorist attacks have been staged against the restaurant and other U.S. corporations perceived to be threatening certain cultures and economies.

country to near collapse. Widespread famine and severe malnourishment of children and adults are common occurrences. The nation depends on foreign food aid. The North Korean government serves its people through the reign of terror and control.

Across the heavily fortified border is South Korea. This country is one of the champions of global economic development. South Korea, too, took full advantage of the possibilities globalization offered in the past two decades. Similarly to neighboring Japan, South Korea is in a group of developed countries with high living standards. Its citizens share freedoms that remain unimaginable to their ethnic counterparts in North Korea. In the case of North Korea, the "bad guy" cannot escape the global community's view. The Communist Party is in complete control. Therefore, it alone must shoulder the blame for the regime's failures and the country's economic woes.

Another country with an oppressive government is Myanmar. The world became painfully aware of the country's political shortcomings soon after it was ravaged by a devastating cyclone (hurricane) in the spring of 2008. Estimates place the death toll as high as one million, with millions more people displaced. Widespread famine and disease added to the human misery. Generals of the ruling military junta, however, were reluctant to allow foreign countries or relief organizations to enter the country to provide desperately needed aid. The regime believed that outsiders would leave and tell the global community how desperate conditions were in the country. Or even worse, they might tell Myanmar's people what freedoms existed beyond their own political borders. The generals simply did not want their political, economic, and social failures to be publicized. They believed that the suppression of truth was far more important than preventing the further loss of human life. For their unwillingness to help their own people, Myanmar's leaders were strongly criticized by the international community. Yet the country survived the crisis and fundamentally, nothing has changed in terms of leadership and governance. After four decades of dictatorship, Myanmar remains an enclosed and impoverished country in which citizens are still terrorized by their own leaders.

Perhaps the most astounding example of government reluctance to accept the impact of globalization is the southern African country of Zimbabwe. The government there turned against its own people. It spread fear and terror by fabricating lies of foreign interference in Zimbabwe's internal affairs. This, in turn, was used by the government as an excuse to crack down on civil liberties. In a period of only several years, Zimbabwe changed from a democratic country that was one of Africa's most prosperous into a nation left in ruins.

Zimbabwe became an independent nation in 1980 and was soon known as the "Breadbasket of Africa." The country was one of few in Africa to have enough food to adequately feed its own people *and* a surplus of grain for export. Following independence, much of the fertile land remained in the hands of farmers of European ancestry. Their ancestors had moved to Zimbabwe when the United Kingdom colonized southern African territories during the nineteenth and twentieth centuries. After generations of living in Africa, most whites, along with their black neighbors, thought of themselves as being loyal Zimbabweans. Relations between whites and blacks were relatively harmonious. Citizens of Zimbabwe enjoyed personal freedoms matched only in a handful of other African countries.

At the turn of the twenty-first century, things began to unravel for Zimbabweans. The political situation worsened beyond repair, taking the country's economy and social structure down with it. The ZANU political party, led by President Robert Mugabe, had been in power since independence, but it faced a serious reelection challenge. In order to solidify its power, the government

MAKING CONNECTIONS

In a globally connected world, great powers share a moral duty to prevent terrorism. But they often fail to do so. Their own interests may not coincide with those of other countries and their policies. When terrorism is an issue, is it wrong for a nation to consider its own interests first? Or should countries follow interests of other nations in crisis? Should the United States have diplomatic relations with countries that, directly or indirectly, support terrorism? What if relations with those countries serve America's own national interests? What active role do you believe the United Nations should play in regard to terrorism? If you were in a decision-making position of power, how would you answer each of these difficult questions?

confiscated successful white-owned farming establishments and redistributed them to its black loyalists. It claimed that the white farmers supported Mugabe's opposition. Many evicted farm owners lost everything. They were forced to leave Zimbabwe, despite their families having lived there for generations. The new landowners were very poorly prepared to step into what had been a modern, commercial agricultural economy. As a result, the country's production of grain and other crops plummeted. Abandoned farms and uncultivated fields soon replaced the former landscape of an African paradise. Almost overnight, Zimbabwe experienced food shortages. Unemployment increased to 80 percent. Even if money was available, the world's highest inflation rate—a whopping 2 million percent!—placed commodities beyond the reach of most citizens. (Imagine an item that cost $1 suddenly costing $2,000,000!) It is little wonder that more than 3 million people have left Zimbabwe in search of a better life elsewhere.

Still, the government continued to provide aid only to its supporters. Any sign of opposition was drastically put down. Citizens who failed to support the Mugabe government were imprisoned, beaten, kidnapped, and even executed. During this entire process, Zimbabwe continued to blame European countries and the United States for its pathetic condition. It put emphasis on fear by creating imaginary enemies who wanted regime change in Zimbabwe. The free flow of information, the key element of globalization, was fiercely suppressed. Any critique of the government, genuine or fabricated, resulted in trials or, as in the case of foreign journalists, expulsion and deportation.

To make conditions worse, Zimbabwe, like the rest of southern Africa, battles a devastating AIDS epidemic. Political and economic disarray has left thousands in dire need of medical attention, but help has yet to arrive. By 2008, the government had even suspended the work of international aid organizations that provided food and medicine to citizens of Zimbabwe. Today the life expectancy in Zimbabwe is under 40, two or three decades less than it should be under normal conditions.

3

SUICIDE BOMBERS

Many people are willing to give their lives for what they believe. They rush barricades in revolutions, fight against foreign occupation, or die preventing the loss of liberties. To die in support of a strongly held belief is the highest honor in many cultures. The United States has a cultural environment in which individualism is emphasized over collectivism. It is easy to forget that focus on the individual is almost exclusively an American cultural trait. The rest of the world favors collectivism in which the needs of society take priority over one's own needs.

Perhaps the most astonishing example of self-sacrifice happened in Ho Chi Min (then Saigon) in 1963 during Vietnam's civil war. The escalation of atrocities between the U.S.-supported South Vietnamese government and the Soviet Union–supported Communist guerrilla Viet Cong left no one safe. South Vietnam's leader, Ngo Dinh Diem, showed little remorse in persecuting Buddhists. Diem, a Roman Catholic, severely suppressed Buddhism in favor of Christianity and associated the Buddhists with antigovernment reactionary forces.

To protest Diem's policy, Buddhist monk Thich Quang Duc arrived at a busy street, splashed his body with gasoline with the help of assistants, and set himself ablaze. A photograph of the burning monk, captured by an Associated Press journalist, circled the world in a matter of hours. Print and electronic media published the photo, which led to widespread condemnation of the treatment of South Vietnamese Buddhists. Under international pressure, Diem's government promised to implement positive changes almost immediately. Although that never happened, Thich Quang Duc managed to expand the global community's interest in South Vietnamese affairs with this sole act.

The idea of suicide by burning or sacrificing oneself in some other way for larger political ideals then spread to the West. Thich Quang Duc inspired individuals in the United States and other countries to give their lives in a similar manner. Several Americans gave their lives in protest against U.S. involvement in the war in Vietnam. Among the most publicized was the 1965 suicide of antiwar activist Norman Morrison in front of the Pentagon. Morrison was a Quaker pacifist who was discouraged by atrocities affecting Vietnamese civilians. He decided to make a political stand in the hope that he would influence decisions to halt the war.

In 1968, Soviet troops invaded Czechoslovakia to stop a threat to Communism. The Communist Party had ruled Czechoslovakia since the end of World War II, and the country was a Soviet satellite (puppet) state. Despite having the status of an independent country, Czech internal affairs were closely monitored by the Soviet government. The voices seeking reform were suppressed. By 1968, the political situation degraded to seriously confrontational levels. Concerned that other satellite states in Eastern Europe would follow Czechoslovakia's path toward reforms, the Soviet Union began to flex its powerful muscles. In August, thousands of troops invaded and occupied Czechoslovakia's capital city of Prague. Frustration over Soviet occupation led Jan Palach, a young Czech, to set himself on fire in Prague's main square. He immediately became the symbol of peaceful resistance throughout Europe as his act was widely reported. Inspired by Palach's suicide, several of his countrymen chose a similar destiny.

Thich Quang Duc's suicide was not a novelty to Asians. Buddhist and Hindu traditions have recorded many similar events in their histories. Yet his message was so powerful because it spread rapidly and reached a vast audience in many countries and cultures. In Europe and North America, such traditions do not exist. A majority of Westerners cannot imagine why someone would choose to die, rather than turning to normal political dialogue. As European and North American history books illustrate, the means of resistance in our culture is to kill others, not ourselves. We see killing oneself for a cause as a foreign and shocking experience. Terrorist organizations have taken notice of the cultural difference.

THE RISE OF SUICIDE BOMBING

One of the largest attacks in Middle Eastern history occurred during the early morning of October 23, 1983. At dawn, two trucks loaded with explosives slammed into barracks occupied by American and French military personnel. The final death count exceeded 300, most of them American Marines. The location was Beirut, the capital city of Lebanon, a small country on the Mediterranean Sea's eastern shores.

International forces arrived in Lebanon to assist in a peacekeeping mission that would bring an end to an ongoing civil conflict between Lebanese factions. The war that ravaged the country was nearing its second decade. It began in 1975 along ethnic and religious lines. Christians and Muslims have lived in Lebanon for centuries, sometimes peacefully and other times engaged in bloody conflict. The country's civil war involved numerous groups, each fighting for its own space or cause. Neighboring countries provided military aid and support to different factions. This outside meddling fueled additional tensions and added to the carnage.

Although a small country, Lebanon is strategically located between Israel and Syria, two adversaries who fought several wars after Israel's independence in 1948. Control over Lebanon and especially over the strategically crucial Bekaa Valley was in both sides' interest. Palestinian militants also operated from southern Lebanon against Israel. This triggered an Israeli intervention and occupation of southern Lebanon in 1982, right in front of Syria's eyes.

Iran also saw Lebanon as a place to spread its influence. In 1979, Iran's power structure was changed by revolution. Religious hard-liners, willing to become serious players in regional geopolitics against the West (specifically against the United States), were now in charge. Iran increased assistance to Lebanese Shia Muslim militias (Iranians are predominantly Shia Muslims, as opposed to Sunni Muslims, who constitute 90 percent of the world's Muslims). The situation in Lebanon was near the point of eruption.

To this day, it remains unsolved who attacked the American and French troops. The two perpetrators who drove the trucks died in the explosions. Speculations about the architects of this brutal attack pointed in the direction of the Lebanese Shia militia, which a few years later became known as Hizbollah. Since then, Hizbollah gradually evolved into a major political and military organization in Lebanon, strong enough to engage in open warfare with Israel and avoid defeat. Throughout the 1980s and until the civil war ended in 1990, Hizbollah conducted scores of actions that included suicide bombings.

The attack of 1983 was not the first of its kind. People sacrificed their lives for similar assignments on many previous occasions. This particular event, however, marked the beginning of an era in which suicide bombings became commonplace in Middle Eastern conflicts. Terrorists realized that with minimal human investment on their own part, they could accomplish

In 1983, a U.S. Marine base in Beirut, Lebanon, was bombed, killing more than 300 people. The event marked the beginning of a new era of terrorist attacks, in which suicide bombing became commonplace.

horrible destruction and loss of life. And it could be done against a better-equipped enemy, one familiar only with conventional methods of fighting. In Middle Eastern urban guerrilla warfare, suicide bombers became widely used. Beneficial in numerous ways, they proved especially useful for their ability to penetrate behind enemy lines.

In expert hands, automobiles and trucks are easily transformed into traveling bombs. They can shift locations if necessary and adjust positions according to their targets. But a suicide bomber wearing an explosive vest is a key weapon associated with Middle Eastern terrorism. Modern plastic explosives are camouflaged under clothing without much difficulty. The explosive vest is strapped around a person's body in a way that is difficult for even a trained eye to detect. A triggering device is within easy reach, so that even if noticed, an attacker can immediately detonate the load.

Knowing that at any given moment a passerby could be a suicide bomber creates immense fear and anxiety among the civilian population. This is precisely why the method is so popular with terrorist organizations. In the Middle East, there is no shortage of volunteers willing to serve as suicide bombers. Most conflicts have religious overtones, and religion is a powerful recruiting tool.

Suicide bombing as a successful terrorist method did not originate in the Middle East. It was the conflict in Sri Lanka that served as an inspiration to terrorists in Lebanon and elsewhere. They integrated techniques from Sri Lanka and further developed their own deadly methods.

DIVINE WIND

Japanese culture places high value on personal honor. To give a life for one's country is considered the highest personal honor and holds a high status in Japanese religious beliefs. During the last part of World War II, the Japanese introduced a suicide bombing technique known as *kamikaze* (meaning "divine wind"). In 1944, the U.S. Navy was approaching the island country. To protect their homeland, Japanese pilots volunteered to crash their fighter planes into approaching battleships, resulting in their own certain deaths.

Rather than trying to deliver bombs and fight American fighter planes, for which advanced piloting skill was necessary, the kamikaze pilot would transform his plane itself into a bomb. Before the war ended, 4,000 mostly inexperienced pilots lost their lives. Most were shot down before they reached their target. The American side suffered serious casualties, as well, but the kamikazes made no impact on the general outcome of the war.

SRI LANKAN CIVIL WAR

Much of the world's attention to suicide bombings is focused on Sunni Muslims. One reason for this association is that al Qaeda is very effective in spreading propaganda. Its members, or affiliated factions, have worldwide connections. Because of al Qaeda's ability to strike in different places, most Westerners assume that suicide bombing is a Muslim invention. Western nations' military engagement and media coverage of the Middle East also contribute to this misconception. Other regional conflicts fail to attract much attention in the Western media. Actually, the birth of modern-era suicide bombings resulted from clashes between Hindu and Buddhist groups in Sri Lanka. Muslims were not involved.

Sri Lanka gained independence (as the Commonwealth of Ceylon) from the United Kingdom in 1948. (The name Sri Lanka was adopted in 1972.) The island country's two largest ethnic groups are the Sinhalese, who make up three-quarters of the population, and the Tamils. The island has other ethnic minorities, including Muslims, but they have not been active in the country's civil conflict.

The relationship between the Sinhalese and Tamils has a history of mistrust and political instability. Occasional periods of calm are frequently interrupted by violence. Under British colonial rule, hostilities between the two groups were not tolerated. Since Sri Lanka gained independence, however, conflict has become commonplace. The Sinhalese majority demanded more rights and used their population dominance to expand their political power. Through a set of reforms and referendums, they minimized Tamil influence in political, economic, and educational circles. In response, Tamil nationalism continued to grow. The Tamils felt that the government relegated them to a position of powerless second-class citizens.

Conditions in Sri Lanka in the 1960s and 1970s mirrored similar issues existing in other parts of Asia and in Africa. Many burning ethnic issues remained unresolved. Unrealistic European-established political boundaries were left for new native governments to sort out. And both political and economic institutions generally failed to bring stability, peace, and development to new nations. The transition to independence was particularly difficult for multiethnic countries.

As an island nation, Sri Lanka did not have to worry about external boundaries. But internal divisions proved to be far more complicated. Sinhalese and Tamils, as is the case with most people in multiethnic countries, have much in common. They shared living space and interacted with one another for centuries. Yet some differences, as minute as they may seem, continued to create a sharp division between the two groups. Sinhalese are of Indo-European descent and practice Buddhism. Tamils are of Dravidian (one of India's aboriginal races) origins, and their religion is Hinduism. They also vary in physical appearance; the Sinhalese being lighter and the Tamils being darker in skin color.

The most significant difference, however, is not so much in religion or race, but in their linguistic background. The Sinhalese and Tamil languages do not share common roots and therefore are not mutually understandable. As a Dravidian language, Tamil is native to southern India and northern Sri Lanka. Sinhalese, an Indo-European tongue, is a relative newcomer to this region. In such circumstances, languages represent a powerful political tool. The Sinhalese majority established their tongue as the country's dominant language. In Tamil eyes, this was a blatant example of the Sinhalese refusal to grant them equal rights.

After years of tensions, the Tamil nationalists became impatient. They had achieved little improvement in their conditions through peaceful political dialogue. Some Tamils responded to the stalemate with calls for a full political separation from the Sinhalese, by violent means if necessary. In the summer of 1983, a civil war erupted in Sri Lanka. The Tamil separatists were greatly outnumbered, and they lacked adequate military equipment such as tanks and planes. Unable to fight by traditional means of warfare, they turned to other methods. For example, they avoided direct combat when possible. Instead, they frequently used guerrilla warfare techniques against government troops. A special team of volunteers was created to conduct dangerous missions behind enemy lines. This was basically a group of militants willing to sacrifice their lives, as the nature of these assignments would lead to almost certain death. A squad of suicide bombers was formed deep in the forests of northeastern Sri Lanka.

Black Tigers

Known as the Black Tigers, the selected group carried out some highly publicized missions that ranged from truck bombings to assassinations of Sinhalese political leaders. In 1993, Sri Lanka's president, Ranasinghe Premadasa, fell victim of a suicide attacker on the streets of Colombo, the capital city. From the beginning, the Black Tigers recruited females for their deadly assignments. In 1991, India's prime minister, Rajiv Gandhi, was assassinated after he greeted a Tamil woman strapped with enough explosives to kill herself, Gandhi, and more than a dozen bystanders.

India's involvement in the Sri Lankan conflict led to a souring relationship between India and the Tamil Black Tigers and, ultimately, to Rajiv Gandhi's assassination. For years, India's government tried to mediate the peacekeeping process, but with little success. India's interest in pushing for peace in Sri Lanka partially stemmed from good intentions. The fact that most ethnic Tamils live in India also influenced India's concern. Furthermore, Tamil separatists in Sri Lanka advocated unification with their ethnic counterparts in India's Tamil Nadu state. Their goal was to form an independent Tamil-dominated country. In that regard, India's involvement in Sri Lanka's internal affairs was also meant to prevent a separatist movement at home. Indian forces were sent to Sri Lanka to keep peace between the Tamils and the Sinhalese. They ended up fighting Tamil Tigers, who responded with Rajiv Gandhi's assassination.

A member of the Tamil Tigers trains Sri Lankan Tamil women in civilian soldiers duty. While terrorist attacks traditionally had been orchestrated and executed by men, the Tamils recognized that women could be much more unexpected and effective.

Tamil Tigers realized early on that with female bombers they could penetrate checkpoints easier and avoid the attention of security forces. Security personnel and bodyguards usually concentrate on males, not females, as potential attackers. This is particularly true in South Asia, where cultural taboos prevent women from interfering with what is traditionally viewed as men's business. The assassination of the prime minister of India certainly was considered such an assignment.

Another cultural tradition helped Gandhi's assassin avoid detection. As a conservative society, India expects Hindu women to dress conservatively and to avoid any expression of "indecency." In traditional terms that means women should always wear a sari, a long cloth wrapped around the body. A sari can be up to ten yards long, but at the same time it is light, silky, and an excellent hiding place for smaller packages such as plastic explosive devices and straps. Detection of someone who carries a deadly weapon that way, particularly on the streets of South Asian cities packed with people, is a difficult task for security forces. Eight years after Rajiv Gandhi's death, Sri Lanka's president, Chandrika Kumaratunga, lost her eye in another attack by the Tamil Tigers. And again, the suicide bomber was a woman.

EXPORT OF DEATH

Middle Eastern militants soon realized that the Tamil Tigers' approach could work on the streets of Israel. Today, as happens frequently in Iraq, female bombers conduct many of the suicide attacks against military units, politicians, and civilians. There, as well, explosives can easily be hidden in traditional female clothing. Religion-based cultural traditions in Southwest Asia require modest clothing and appearance. Islam requires women

MAKING CONNECTIONS

Western countries are proud of the individual liberties they offer their residents. Their goal is to export Western freedoms to the rest of the world. But there is a problem: the issue of racial and ethnic profiling of immigrants. Those newcomers possibly having ties to terrorist organizations are increasingly publicized in Europe and North America. In times of crisis, should nations be allowed to sacrifice the rights of some residents in order to protect their citizens? Should they be able to maintain tighter security even if it means scrutinizing people on the basis of their race, religion, ethnicity, or gender for the purpose of the common good?

to dress in a way that does not reveal their bodies. That is, their dresses should serve as loose covers. In even more conservative areas, women often wear *burkas*, gowns that cover the entire body, including the head. There is only a small opening around the eyes.

Recruitment of female suicide bombers is a model of global connections at work. Islamic terrorists apply methods identical to that of the Tamil Tigers. Yet the two groups are fundamentally different. Muslim terrorists follow their religious platform to justify brutal ways of engagement. They have to assess and manipulate religious beliefs to fit the agenda of not only killing others, but of recruiting women to do so. Radical Islamists usually practice religious beliefs that fail to promote female rights and equality. In plain words, they believe men should fight wars and women should stay at home and raise future warriors.

The Tamil Tigers are an organization driven by secular values. Hinduism is not a key factor behind Tamil separatism. Rather, Socialistic ideals and classless values are some of the primary aspects in their political platform. Socialist ideology advocates gender equality as one of its main goals. This explains why female Tamil Tigers were allowed to plan and execute attacks with their male comrades.

As a political ideology, Socialism is not native to Sri Lanka. Major left-wing political ideologies, including Socialism and Communism, originated in nineteenth-century Europe. From there they gradually spread worldwide. Fascism, too, as a right-wing ideology, found its way out of Europe to other regions. The two acted as barriers to democracy, but when they crashed against each other, escalation of terrorism reached some of the highest levels in the modern era. The following chapter provides examples of left-wing and right-wing terrorism, both past and present.

4

TERRORISM AND POLITICAL IDEOLOGIES

Fundamentally, "left-wing" views are liberal. They seek change. Advocates of "right-wing" policies are conservative. They seek to maintain existing conditions. Extreme forms of both viewpoints usually are practiced by small but vocal groups of supporters. As a rule, radicals do not win elections because voters prefer middle-of-the-road options. Thus, in order to promote their agendas and attract new membership, radicals often turn to violence. Violent extremism generally is not old people's business. It tends to be a young and energetic crowd who seek an immediate change to the existing political conditions. They are the ones willing to die, or to kill, for their beliefs.

Communism and Fascism are two quite opposite belief systems. Communists advocate collective ownership of everything the state possesses. In the Fascist system, power is concentrated in the hands of a few or a single dictator. Freedom for alternative political choices in both systems is quite limited. Opposition views are drastically suppressed. Individual rights are replaced by the rights of the state. In practical terms that means that a small social elite holds control over many aspects of the lives of average people. Both ideologies, as history has recorded, could not function without oppression and violence. Communists have used violence to gain power, and Fascists have used it to preserve their existing power. Their interactions have led to many violations of civil rights.

REVOLUTION AS THE ANSWER

In the 1960s, the generation known as the baby boomers was coming of age in Europe and North America. Born in the 1940s, they were a generation that sought to change the world quickly. But they failed to remember how difficult it is to have change without conflict. Radical elements benefited from young people's energy. Leftist policies and calls for Communist revolution attracted many, especially college students. Universities became hotbeds of leftist radicalism. Many students were inspired by the writings of Chinese Communist leader Mao Tse-tung and the actions of Argentine revolutionary Ernesto "Che" Guevara. Across the Western world, colleges served as headquarters of political dissent. Debates about political and social issues echoed in student cafeterias. Most organizations advocated a Socialist society, but one achieved through peaceful means. Nonetheless, there were many who believed that violence was the only way to achieve a new society.

The 1960s—an era of the "Peace" generation—proved to be a decade of conflict. The 1961 Cuban Missile Crisis brought the United States and the Soviet Union to the brink of nuclear confrontation. In order to strengthen ties with the Cuban Communist regime, the Soviets provided military assistance to this Caribbean nation. Among the military hardware were missiles that carried nuclear warheads. The idea of having such an arsenal only 90 miles (145 kilometers) from American soil posed a huge problem for newly elected U.S. president John F. Kennedy.

After a tense series of discussions, a diplomatic solution eventually was reached and the threat of war subsided.

A few years later, American intervention in Indochina escalated Vietnam's civil war. At home, riots and protests against the war were widespread. In the Middle East, Israel victoriously confronted several Arab nations in the 1967 Six Days' War. The following year, Soviet troops marched into Czechoslovakia. In addition to these events, the decade experienced many civil and regional conflicts, some of which erupted into heated warfare.

In modern history, 1968 is remembered as the turning point. Students entered the streets of Paris, Rome, Mexico City, and other capitals. Some set clear goals, while others simply channeled their accumulated energy. In France, students inspired unions and workers who initiated a strike that paralyzed the country for weeks. Mexico City's security forces killed several hundred student protesters. The United States could not avoid social unrest either. During the Democratic Party's National Convention in Chicago, antiwar riots broke out in front of television cameras. Two decades after the end of World War II, the new generation was on the streets demanding change. Some demonstrators hoped for a student-inspired international movement that would fight against injustice and work actively against imperialism.

Historically, the political pendulum swung in another direction, and the goals of young radical revolutionaries were never reached. Left-wing movements fragmented into numerous factions. In the West, the movement failed; the hoped-for revolution never happened. By the end of the decade, Che Guevara was captured and executed in Bolivia. Bolivians wanted no part of the revolution that he hoped to start there. At the same time, Mao's government in China was terrorizing its own people. The Cultural Revolution, aimed to preserve China's Communist principles, ended with millions of Chinese either dead or imprisoned. Mao's stature as the moral leader of all Communists, just like Joseph Stalin's a decade earlier, was tainted forever. Ideological leaders who could unify the Left were now gone.

What events of the 1960s did achieve was to plant seeds for future revolutions. Many revolutionaries of the 1970s and later were inspired by events of the 1960s. Much of the left-wing terrorism of the twenty-first century was built on the 1960s foundation. And, as the Tamil separatist movement illustrates, it will not disappear for some time.

RISE OF RIGHT-WING TERRORISM

Two types of terrorist activity are conducted by extreme right-wing groups: government-sponsored and independent enterprises. Fascistic and pro-Fascistic regimes use many methods to spread and preserve fear among the political opposition and among ordinary citizens. These regimes sometimes act openly. But more often they rely on covert operations conducted by assigned teams. This makes it more difficult to pin wrongdoings on the government.

In covert programs, those who commit acts of terror are not claimed by the government for which they secretly are working. If caught, they cannot reveal the agency for whom they work. Kidnappings, torture, murder, and sabotage are their most common tools. So-called death squads are an example of this covert approach. The squads are paramilitary organizations. They receive guidance, training, and equipment support from the government and military, but they take action independently. Outside government-sponsored right-wing terrorist circles, many organizations run their businesses independent of government and politicians.

Many extremists concentrate on a single social or cultural issue. For example, the Ku Klux Klan spread across the American South in the second part of the nineteenth century. They advocated white supremacy, Protestantism, and segregation. In their early days, Klansmen had close connections with and even support from many powerful politicians. Some members held high legislative, executive, and judiciary offices. Even a chief justice of the United States Supreme Court, Hugo Black, had previous connections with the Klan.

Today, right-wing extremists in the United States tend to be marginalized fanatics in a fight for some cause. Because their views are not those of mainstream Americans, they become frustrated. Unable to achieve their goals politically, they may engage in acts of hatred and terror. Most of today's Klan supporters are younger males who feel angry and isolated. Unable to succeed in mainstream society, they join a community of like-minded people. Such individuals form the membership of skinhead and neo-Nazi groups in the United States and Europe.

There are also armed militias whose activities are not necessarily directed against a particular racial, religious, or ethnic group. They are in revolt against a country's government. In the United States, where the Second Amendment of the Constitution allows individuals to possess firearms, fully armed private militias are not uncommon. The majority of them do not engage in any direct conflict with the federal government. Rather, they work on expanding anti-government propaganda and hold exercises on privately owned compounds. Disappointment with political decisions at the federal level is typically a driving force behind such groups. Several high-profile acts of terrorism in the United States were committed by individuals with ties to right-wing militias.

ATTACK ON AMERICA FROM THE INSIDE

The most devastating U.S. attack committed by domestic terrorists was the 1996 Oklahoma City bombing. One early spring morning, a massive truck bomb exploded in front of the Alfred P. Murrah Federal Building in downtown Oklahoma City. The final death toll reached 168, with three times as many wounded. This was the highest number of casualties on American soil from a terrorist's bomb. The nation watched in shock when the two conspirators, Timothy McVeigh and Terry Nichols, were revealed to

Neo-Nazis, or "skinheads," around the world believe in the supremacy of the white race. Like the Ku Klux Klan and other extreme right-wing groups, many neo-Nazis have engaged in acts of terror designed to intimidate and suppress minority groups in an effort to preserve their own race and culture.

be U.S. citizens. In fact, McVeigh was a decorated veteran of the 1991 Gulf War, in which U.S.-led coalition forces liberated Kuwait from Iraq's occupation.

After renting a truck in Junction City, Kansas, the two conspirators loaded it with a huge fertilizer-based bomb. Most materials were readily available for purchase in stores. McVeigh drove the truck to Oklahoma City and executed the deadly operation. Among the victims were many children, because the building had a busy day-care center. With a stroke of luck, a state trooper arrested McVeigh within hours of the attack on an interstate highway near the Oklahoma–Kansas border. He was pulled over because the license plates had been removed from the vehicle he was driving. Additionally, McVeigh was carrying a concealed firearm for which he did not have a permit. After hearing about McVeigh's arrest, Nichols surrendered to Kansas authorities. After a lengthy trial, McVeigh received a death sentence and was executed in federal prison in Terre Haute, Indiana. Nichols is currently serving a life sentence. The FBI conducted a thorough investigation of the attack but learned little. The reason McVeigh and Nichols turned to terrorism may never be known. It is known, however, that both held strong right-wing views and were in close contact with extremist groups.

Of particular interest to the FBI was McVeigh's connection with the Elohim City settlement in eastern Oklahoma. Elohim City is not a real city, but a compound in an unassuming marginal area of rural Oklahoma located near the Arkansas border. On a daily basis, not much is going on in this part of the state, a condition that residents of the compound prefer. Founded by religious fundamentalists in the 1970s, this place often serves as an isolated refuge for right-wing extremists. Visitors range from white supremacists, survivalists, and Klansmen, to skinhead and neo-Nazi types and members of paramilitary organizations. Sometimes even bank robbers and other outlaws seek refuge there. Feelings against the federal government are very strong in Elohim City.

It was clear that McVeigh harbored strong feelings against the federal government and its role in what he perceived as an attack on Americans' liberties; he was outraged at the FBI's attack on the Branch Davidians, a fundamentalist religious sect. Two years earlier, almost 80 members of this group perished at their compound in Waco, Texas, when it was set ablaze. McVeigh, it was believed, responded violently because of a desire to avenge the Waco tragedy.

McVeigh also possessed *The Turner Diaries*. This was a novel, written in the 1970s by a white supremacist, about the revolution against the federal government and subsequent elimination of all non-whites. Some consider *The Turner Diaries* to be an unofficial

THE WEATHER UNDERGROUND

Compared to other regions of the world, the United States has suffered little from left-wing terrorism. The most significant terrorist threat came from the group of leftist extremists called the Weatherman. The small group, numbering several dozen members, was responsible for a series of bombings during the early 1970s. Their goal was to initiate Communist revolution in the United States. They tried to overthrow the capitalist government aggressively, rather than by peaceful means that would take much longer to achieve results. The organization went into hiding to avoid prosecution and became known as the Weather Underground. Despite many bombings, they were careful to destroy only property and avoid human casualties. Targets were usually buildings occupied by government authorities or the military. On one occasion, they even managed to plant a bomb inside of the Pentagon!

As the Vietnam War wound down and American troops pulled out, the Weatherman's mission lost its major driving force. The international revolution never happened, and in the following years the Weather Underground gradually disbanded. The members surrendered to police and received mostly minor punishments.

handbook and source of guidance for militant right-wing extremists. On the day of the attack, McVeigh carried several pages from the book.

Finally, the date of the bombing appeared to have been carefully chosen. The Oklahoma City explosion occurred on April 19. That date was significant to McVeigh for two reasons. First, the date was the second anniversary of the destruction of the Branch Davidians' compound in deadly flames after the long siege. Even more revealing was a little-publicized event that occurred in Arkansas on the day of the Oklahoma City bombing. On April 19, 1995, a white racist named Robert Snell was executed for killing a pawn-shop owner in Texarkana a decade earlier. In the early 1980s, Snell also planned to attack the very same Alfred P. Murrah Federal Building in Oklahoma City. Before the execution, Snell indicated that his death was going to be avenged and the federal government would pay a stern price.

On the day of the execution, in fulfillment of one of his last wishes, he asked to watch television news at the same time as the Oklahoma City explosion. This certainly was an unusual request for someone about to be executed! For many years, Snell had maintained close connections with the Elohim City crowd. McVeigh knew Snell and other residents of Elohim City.

Terrorist connections between McVeigh and others were difficult to prove beyond a reasonable doubt. No one from Elohim City was ever prosecuted by the U.S. government. Unless they want to implicate others, terrorists are skillful in erasing connections between themselves and their support network. In McVeigh's case, all such possible links were erased as though they never existed. But in almost every conspiracy theory, there is at least a small grain of truth.

THE LATIN AMERICAN EXPERIENCE

Latin America, primarily Colombia, is a region where left-wing terrorism still holds significant ground. The Revolutionary Armed

Forces of Colombia–People's Army (FARC) is the most influential terrorist (to its adversaries) or guerrilla (to its supporters) force in the Western Hemisphere. It has operated from deep within Colombia's tropical rain forests for almost a half century.

FARC was formed by Colombia's Communist Party in the 1960s. Its primary task was to resist what the Communists believed to be the exploitation of Colombia's poor. Initially, its goal was to topple the rule of the wealthy minority, whose land and other wealth was to be taken and redistributed to poor rural (and mostly aboriginal) peasants. In this regard, FARC's goals did not differ from most other Latin American guerrilla groups. They primarily fought for land reforms and social justice. Most such groups established bases in the countryside where sanctuary, supplies, and local support were all easier to obtain.

Until recently, democracy was a foreign idea to most Latin Americans. The political process in this culture region almost always included smoking gun barrels. Transitions of power came from revolutions and military coups. For centuries, power was concentrated in the hands of wealthy families of Spanish origin who had acquired the land during the colonial period. The Amerindian (American Indian) population was largely poor and powerless. In such a rigid socioeconomic system, it was difficult if not impossible for them to get ahead.

Amerindians are the population majority in much of Middle America and the Andean countries. Traditionally, they have been a highly marginalized people who receive few government benefits. The alternative to poverty has been to join antigovernment guerrilla forces, such as FARC. Few people had any idea what Communism or Socialism were in philosophical terms. But they all understood calls for land reforms and equality. Movements similar to that in Colombia appeared in El Salvador, Peru, Nicaragua, and elsewhere, creating bitter and long-lasting conflicts.

Today the picture looks different. Following the end of the Cold War, leftists in Latin America lost the Soviet Union's sponsorship. Revolutions such as that in Cuba never appeared less attractive than in the early 1990s. As Socialism and Communism lost their impact worldwide, the quality of life and economic development steadily increased in Latin America. Democracy gradually spread throughout the region. A number of former revolutionaries became political representatives, even freely elected presidents, rather than fight from the forest. FARC's numbers dwindled, but it managed to survive by shifting its focus to other issues.

Although they still number in the thousands, current FARC members show more concern about their own survival than about achieving original revolutionary goals. They are very active in international illegal drug trafficking. (Colombia produces a majority of global supplies of cocaine.). FARC members also are involved in numerous assassinations and kidnappings, both for extortion and prisoner exchange. Although its membership has dwindled, FARC continues to exist. The key to its survival is the understanding that to fight locally it needs to operate globally. The drug trade is a lucrative business, so cocaine produced in Colombia under FARC's oversight is transported to the United States and elsewhere.

Profits from the drug trade are used to purchase weapons from international dealers and to bring foreign terrorist experts to Colombia to educate FARC in training and combat. In 2001, for example, several Irishmen, members of the Provisional IRA (a leftist branch of the Irish Republican Army) traveled to Colombia to provide their expertise in bomb making. In 2008, the major figure in international arms trafficking was detained in Bangkok, Thailand. He was under suspicion of trying to arrange a weapons shipment to FARC.

OPERATION CONDOR AND THE DEATH SQUADS

Throughout Latin America's history, the rule of law always occupied a secondary position to the rule of power. And, of course, those in positions of power were the ones who created the laws.

Rightist regimes ruled with iron fists, and they tried to prevent loss of power by all means necessary. Their response to the leftist revolutionaries, and other critics of the government, was often terrorism. Suppression of leftists became an intergovernmental South American project in the mid-1970s under the name Operation Condor. The program involved the cooperation of South American right-wing dictatorships in creating a continental force to fight their Communist enemies. (Note: South America is a continent that begins at Colombia's border with Panama; Latin America is the culture region that extends southward from the U.S.–Mexico boundary.)

During the 1970s, South America was in a major state of transition. Economic woes spread throughout the continent, bringing hyperinflation and unemployment. Frustration with political regimes grew to an explosive level. There were few reforms that held hope of jump-starting national economies. The situation was equally grim in regard to social issues. Dictatorial social policies further increased dissatisfaction with political leaders. Yet hope for creating a productive political environment remained a remote dream. Existing leaders feared the loss of power if reforms were adopted. As a result, they harshly suppressed any and all forms of opposition. They were particularly wary of what had happened following Chile's election of Salvador Allende. Faced with these concerns, the South American dictators decided to develop a plan.

Operation Condor informally began with the collaboration between Chilean and Argentinean intelligence agents. In Chile, political dissidents started to disappear immediately after General Augusto Pinochet and colleagues conducted the coup in 1973. Pinochet's reign over Chile would last almost two decades. During his time in office, few people dared to publicly express their leftist views. Three years later, the Argentinean military assumed power in another illegal intervention and immediately abolished democracy. Its secret service units approached the country's political issues in a fashion similar to Chile's.

Argentina and Chile worked together closely on the exchange of intelligence information and on neutralizing those they considered to be a threat to national security. Neighboring Brazil, Uruguay, Paraguay, and Bolivia eventually joined this secret terrorist program. Others such as Colombia, Venezuela, and Peru now are known to have been participants, but they were involved to a lesser degree.

It is difficult to know the exact number of victims of government oppression during this time. Estimates range in the tens of thousands. Intimidation included basic imprisonment for the lucky ones and abductions, torture, and executions for the less fortunate. Thousands simply vanished. Bodies of the vanished often would suddenly reappear on streets or in garbage dumps to serve as an example to others. The entire continent was kept in fear. In Argentina alone, hundreds of children were taken away from their ill-fated parents. Their destinies varied. Some were left on the streets or placed in orphanages. Others were given to military officers' families to raise them as their own.

Leftist activists, their sympathizers, and journalists had the most to fear. They represented a direct threat to the regimes. Many of their relatives, as well, disappeared, never to be seen again. The guilt-by-perceived-association was punishable by death. Operation Condor had all the characteristics of a global program. Many dissidents outside of South America, but with ties to the continent, were assassinated.

The United States did little to prevent this kind of terrorism in its backyard. To understand America's passiveness, the political "climate" of the 1970s must be recalled. The Cold War was raging. To the United States, it was essential to have peaceful conditions in South America. Therefore, despite their extreme measures, vocally anti-Communist military juntas were welcomed by Washington. They were a preferred option to pro–Soviet Union leftist regimes such as Allende's.

We will probably never know how involved the United States was in Operation Condor. Certainly U.S. intelligence agencies, such as the CIA, knew about the operation's intentions and methods. Ever since 1823, Americans have kept a close eye on Latin American affairs. That year, President James Monroe (1817–1825) presented his famous doctrine. The Monroe Doctrine stated that no European power could intervene in the Western Hemisphere without America's approval. If such would indeed occur, the United States had an obligation to protect its geopolitical interests. The Monroe Doctrine became increasingly important during the Cold War. It was used on numerous occasions to justify U.S. military intervention and support for Latin American anti-Communist regimes.

General Augusto Pinochet orchestrated a coup that effectively abolished democracy in Chile. During Pinochet's reign, political dissidents began to disappear, and citizens were prevented from expressing leftist views. *Above*, family members of people who disappeared during Pinochet's reign demonstrate in 2004.

Operation Condor relied on death squads. Death squads were usually small groups of unidentified men. They were secretly affiliated with military, police, and other local authorities who provided them with the freedom to act on their own. Under the darkness of night, individuals or entire families could disappear at the hands of unknown assailants. Official investigations of crimes usually went nowhere. Cases were blamed on common criminals and were rapidly forgotten.

Operation Condor lasted for several years. In the early 1980s, however, South American geopolitical circumstances entered another phase that hastened its end. Argentinean junta leaders made a mistake in 1982 by starting a war against the United Kingdom over the Falkland Islands. This small group of islands is of little economic, population, political, or other importance. Geographically, the islands are closest to Argentina, which claims them politically as its own Malvinas Islands. Yet, they

MAKING CONNECTIONS

Capital punishment is a controversial and heated topic in today's world. Terrorists operate across many political boundaries. For example, they may be citizens of one country and residents of another. Their attacks may be planned in still another nation. Then they may travel through several other countries en route to the country in which they plan to carry out their attack. Which country should have jurisdiction over their terrible act(s)? The terrorists may face the death penalty in one country. Yet in another nation, where executions are not allowed, they may receive only a lengthy prison sentence. Finally, in a country that unofficially approves of their actions, they may be received as heroes. How would you work to resolve this issue and create a global agreement on terrorism? Who should have jurisdiction over such crimes? What should the punishment be for terrorist acts in which fatalities result?

remained a British colony for centuries. In the short-lived war, Argentinean forces invaded the Falklands and lost. The defeat crippled the junta's leadership and helped to create conditions ripe for its ousting in 1983. This was the beginning of the end for the international web of government-sponsored terrorism in South America. Other regional dictatorships also gradually faded. By the turn of the twenty-first century, Latin American right-wing juntas had become but a grim memory.

THE LEGACY OF DEATH SQUADS

Death squads have existed throughout human history in various forms and for different intentions. But the South American experience established this form of terrorism as an activity with strong global connections. Clearly, it reflected the interests of two foreign powers, the Soviet Union and the United States. Further, it inspired others around the world to apply a similar approach.

Operation Condor and its death squads became a model not only for protecting the existing power structure, but also for ethnic, religious, and other conflicts. During the 1980s, a bitter civil war broke out in the Central American country of El Salvador. Death squads murdered thousands of civilians. In 1993, a genocide started in the small African country of Rwanda. In a period of several months, small groups of machete-wielding Hutu tribesmen massacred nearly a million Tutsis, all of them fellow Rwandans. Culturally, Hutus and Tutsis are almost identical peoples. For that reason, one would expect them to live in harmony. Yet they have a long history of mutual antagonism. That year, militant Hutus first orchestrated an assassination of Rwanda's leader. Then they set in motion the genocide of Tutsis and also fellow Hutus who were unwilling to cooperate in the slaughter of their neighbors. Most recently, armed groups have attacked villages in western Sudan's Darfur province, where they use tactics of murder and rape against residents.

5

MILITANT ISLAM

Terrorism in Southwest Asia, the cultural heart of Islam, receives ample exposure in the international media. Hardly a day passes without news reports about some terrorist activity in that region. The electronic and printed media bombard the public with horror stories of rocket attacks, car bombings, assassinations, and kidnappings. To an outside viewer it seems that violence is just a part of everyday life in this region. And, as a matter of fact, it is.

The history of Southwest Asia has been chaotic. Peaceful transitions of power have been rare. For males, dying by the sword has been much more likely than from natural means. Oppression of commoners in order to extract benefits for the ruling few was, and still is, a part of the natural way of governing. Rulers also were considered the ultimate owners of the land and the people who lived on it. Historically, this situation played out—perhaps with slightly different themes—throughout much of the world.

Medieval European kings, for example, enjoyed absolute power to act as they wished. Most of them took advantage of their power and ruled over their subjects with an iron fist. It took many revolutions, wars, and millions of lives lost for Europeans to reach their current political arrangement. The United States, as well, was built on the revolution against the British monarchy that lasted for years and took many lives. But in the West this kind of behavior happened decades and centuries ago. Conditions have changed radically since then.

The French Revolution was the turning point in European history. It abolished the tradition of monarchy and created a republic in which people enjoyed freedom and liberty. The revolution's leading figures believed that France's citizens should have the right to participate in political affairs. Yet it was they who first used the word *terror* in reference to the brutality of this period. By the end of the eighteenth century, France had drifted from its earlier republican ideas. Napoleon Bonaparte had become the country's strong-arm ruler. Decades would pass before the country returned to a democratic path.

Political transitions are cultural transitions, and the people need time to absorb changes and adjust to new conditions. It cannot happen overnight. France took nearly two centuries to establish a sound democracy. It is only natural that regions with little exposure to democracy would lag in the speed of political transition.

COLLECTIVE MEMORY

Southwest Asia's history is one of almost continuous turbulence. When people there talk about past times, it is much easier to remember conflicts than peaceful periods. This burden of selective historical memory is a force that perpetuates future conflicts. We cannot easily understand such an attitude. Americans and Canadians, after all, generally are oriented toward the future. With each new generation, our collective historical memory fades even more. Baby boomers of the 1960s worried little about the Second World War. Those who grew up during the 1980s had little memory of how deeply the nation was affected by the war in Vietnam. Even the Cold War seems like ancient history to most of us.

Generalizations like these illustrate how rapidly our society moves into a new era while leaving the past behind as a vague and distant memory. In the West, emphasis is on the individual as the center of society. This contributes to the notion that the future holds more importance than the past. An obsession with the past, however, can hinder socioeconomic gain. The general social environment leaves plenty of room for personal decisions and choices. Basically, we are free to do what we want, rather than what society expects from us based on our ethnicity or religion.

American and Canadian societies include a rich mosaic of individuals and viewpoints. Yet we are governed by the same general sets of rules that also offer equal rights and protections to minority groups. The United States was created as an idea to which people of diverse backgrounds were drawn and voluntarily joined together. It was an alternative and yet successful way of creating a new nation. Generally speaking, most countries are created by people who share cultural ties, mostly through common ancestry. They want to be politically separated from others who do not share their history, values, and way of life.

In Southwest Asia, the memory of past times is what holds people together. They are united by a sense of belonging to a larger collective unit such as a tribe or a nation. It is essential to do so in a region composed of so many different cultural groups. Some of them track tribal origins back thousands of years. They cherish tradition and independence and look at the past as the key experience in learning how to survive today. Elders use history and tradition to etch the importance of tribal identity in each new generation's minds. Learning the culture's rules and ways assures the continuation of a group's existence. Tribes and clans are designed to work as survival mechanisms. They allow individuals to exist under the protection of a larger unit. One of the strongest tools in maintaining the collective memory is religion.

An individual's lifestyle must align with the interests of the entire group. An Arab farmer faces grim prospects in drought years if he fails to help fellow tribesmen. A Bedouin (Arab pastoral nomad) cannot remain one without the support of his kin. Understandably, then, each individual in this region is a member of a particular group. And members must cooperate with one another to support the group and their own kin. This kind of group unity creates a strong "us" versus "them" relationship with outsiders. It is a condition that often leads to conflict within Southwest Asia's multiethnic environment. Developing a sense of regional unity is all but impossible when each individual tribal group promotes its own interests. In addition, many political boundaries were imposed by European colonial powers and in no way reflect local geographic realities. Consequently, Southwest Asia is often little more than a pawn in a global geopolitical struggle over which it has little if any influence. Being home to the world's richest petroleum deposits adds to the region's turmoil. It is little wonder that Southwest Asia is a hotbed of terrorism.

CONTEMPORARY IRAQ

Iraq is a splendid example of the foregoing conditions. At the dawn of the twentieth century, it was a province of the Ottoman Empire. When the Turkish-ruled empire disintegrated after the end of World War I, the British gained control over Iraq. The relationship between Iraqis and Turks was uneasy. The British also expected unrest, and to calm the region they installed the local strongman, Faisal, as king. In 1932, Iraq gained independence. That effectively established a Hashemite dynasty (the Hashemite tribal line began with the prophet Muhammad in the seventh century), which ruled Iraq until 1959. Hashemites, who had close ties with the West, attempted to modernize the country. But they faced strong resistance from religious groups.

In 1959, after many failed attempts, the Hashemite monarchy finally was overthrown. In revenge, many of its supporters were killed. During the following decades, Iraq experienced several other violent changes of government. Each transition included the execution or imprisonment of tribal and religious leaders affiliated with "disloyal" elements. It was in this setting that Saddam Hussein assumed the presidency. He successfully used tribal affiliations and loyalties in creating a government and security forces. After rising to power, Hussein quickly executed anyone perceived as a threat. Then he installed relatives and fellow tribal members to hold vital positions in the military and the government. Without them he could not hold power and, of course, without him they would be powerless.

Hussein, a Sunni Muslim, promoted members of friendly Sunni tribes in a similar way. He needed their support because his own tribe was a small minority group in the country of more than 20 million people. Members of untrustworthy Sunni tribes, other religions (Shia), or ethnic groups (Kurds) were kept under strict control. Any actions that Hussein's government believed to be threatening were dealt with harshly.

In 1988, Iraq's military attacked Kurdish settlements along the Iranian border. Chemical weapons (which are weapons of mass destruction) killed thousands of civilians during the Iran–Iraq War (1980–1988). As the war progressed and Iraqis kept losing battles, the Kurds sided with the Iranians. Hussein's government saw this as a threat. Several years later, after Iraq's loss in the Gulf War (1991), a Shia uprising in the southern provinces was ended in an equally brutal way. Although Shia Muslims form the majority of Iraq's population, they were forcefully subdued during Hussein's rule. This uprising was their attempt to achieve more freedom. But Saddam Hussein applied Southwest Asia's traditional method of power preservation: The dead cannot fight, and the living must be kept on a tight leash.

In 2003, Saddam Hussein and his supporters saw their luck turn. His powerful Sunnis lost rule over Iraq after the country fell under American occupation. This time, Iraq's Shia Muslims took over. The sudden change in status led many Sunni tribal leaders and their kinsmen to rebel. They fought bitterly against the Americans and also against the Shia with equally brutal vengeance. Insurgents employed various terrorist methods to generate fear among Shia. Bombings, executions, and forceful removal of entire neighborhoods reminded the world of the ethnic cleansing in the early 1990s in Bosnia and Herzegovina. The prospect of civil war loomed over the country. Many Sunnis initially supported the insurgents. They feared that Iraqi Shia were

In April 2003, U.S. Marines toppled a statue of Iraqi president Saddam Hussein during the Fall of Baghdad. Thus ended the reign of the murderous tyrant, who was captured, tried, and executed.

eager to do the same to them that Saddam Hussein had done to the Shia.

As has happened many times before, all sides of the conflict looked back in their own history and realized that sides had to be taken in order for their own kin to survive. After all, Sunni and Shia Muslims have been in different stages of conflict since the seventh century. Thus, the current alignment along sectarian and tribal lines was the only option for individual and group survival. Historical experience tells Iraqis that the only possible way to survive is if one holds power over others in the way that Hussein controlled "disloyal" Iraqis. Thus far, however, Iraq has miraculously managed to avoid an explosive civil war that would destroy the country.

THE ROLE OF RELIGION IN THE MUSLIM WORLD

The world's great religions evolved gradually and over centuries to become what they are today. Each of them has faced many attempts at "reform" (change). Christianity has undergone many changes. So have Judaism and Hinduism. Buddhism, another among the leading religions, began as a Hindu reform movement.

What all religions have in common is that they offer a set of cultural rules designed for people to follow. That is, already existing moral codes, values, customs, and traditions were brought into the institution of religion. When Moses stood in front of the Jews and delivered the Ten Commandments, he was not introducing anything new to his people. The commandments were ancient moral values grouped together. Moses only put them together in order to reinforce traditional values and to create unity among Jews. Islam's experience in that matter is no different than Christianity's or Judaism's, the other two great monotheistic (belief in one God) religions of Southwest Asia.

What the prophet Muhammad did was to organize a set of norms to regulate an unstable and often violent society. The

Arabian Peninsula in the seventh century was a collection of warring Bedouin tribes. Through blood feuds, kidnappings, and thieving, local warlords fought for power through their mercenaries' swords. The deserts of Arabia were a folk-culture (traditional society) environment where the unwritten law of the land was a mixture of ancient traditions and various pagan beliefs. Killing to preserve family honor, arranged marriage, and absolute male dominance already existed there long before the introduction of Islam.

Among the most important folk-culture traits is a belief in multiple gods, or polytheism, which was widely held throughout the Arabian Peninsula. Muhammad decided to incorporate these, and many other cultural elements, into a new system that would worship only a single deity, Allah. It was a radical step at that time, and Muhammad and his early followers faced many obstacles. They managed, however, to survive. By the end of the seventh century, Islam had become a large and rapidly growing faith. It had expanded throughout much of Southwest Asia and across North Africa.

Islam means "submission to a single God." Muslims believe that God dictated words to Muhammad, and that they are recorded in the holy book, the Qur'an. Theological debate aside, it is clear that many elements of Arabic folk culture are incorporated into Islamic teachings. Muhammad was quite successful in reforming his society in a way similar to that of some Christian and Jewish reformers. Moving forward fifteen centuries, we can now understand why such a close relationship exists between Islam and the traditional moral codes in this part of the world. Islam of the seventh century is a product of the local folk culture of the time. Thus, even today, Muslims must follow the word of God that is recorded word for word in the Qur'an. In so doing, they face the challenge of adapting seventh century folkways to a twenty-first-century lifestyle.

Trying to blend the old traditions with the realities of contemporary living creates a serious moral dilemma for many Muslims. The word of Allah cannot be updated at will to serve the social and cultural purposes of the twenty-first century and the demands of postindustrial society. Culture and society have changed greatly since the seventh century. Moral dilemmas that arise from this intellectual conflict among Muslims create fuel for the flame of terrorism. For example, terrorists claim that modernization ("Westernization") is a deliberate attempt to destroy core Muslim cultural values. Acceptance of the modern traits would replace ancient cultural values, many of which are incorporated in the Qur'an. If that happens, many argue, Islam may simply cease to exist. Commenting on the difference between freedom of speech and promotion of religious hatred against Muslims, one Muslim leader noted, "Islam is a big part of the identity of Muslims, so if you attack Islam it is for us the same as attacking and discriminating against Muslims."

It is on grounds such as these that terrorist networks justify their agendas and call for *jihad* (holy war) to prevent the destruction of Islam. The war against invading enemies of Islam is in their view a defensive measure, and is therefore justified. Osama bin Laden has repeatedly called for the spread of terrorism to protect Islam. One of his main arguments has been that the American military presence in Saudi Arabia is in preparation for an attack on the Muslim holy land by the Western infidels.

SEPARATION OF CHURCH AND STATE

A discussion about culture as a whole and the role of Islam as an important culture trait would not be complete without reference to the relation between Islam and politics in Southwest Asia. Separation of church and state, as it is known in the West, is a foreign and unnatural notion to Islam. The purpose of Islam is to serve as a set of norms for the entire society. These guidelines cannot exclude social or political matters. A religious leader's duty is to serve his community and to provide spiritual guidance on the basis of Islamic beliefs and traditions. This means that *all* aspects of life in Islamic society should be derived from religion.

Any influence that is not approved by religious leaders should be avoided by society. Such a system is rigid because it is the rigidity that keeps the system in place.

A historical example of a similar system was set in medieval Europe. The Roman Catholic clergy's influence extended far beyond the cathedrals' pews. The pope was more politically influential than kings. Many wars, including the Crusades, were fought in the name of religion. Popes justified their aspirations as being God's will because they were God's representatives on Earth. A Medieval papal state existed and spread across a good portion of the Italian Peninsula. The Roman Catholic Church eventually relinquished its political aspirations, but rather unwillingly and after many centuries of struggle. It still remains

ASSASSINS

An assassination is a killing for political gain. It owes its name to the medieval religious sect, Hashshashin, that perfected the method. At the end of the eleventh century, as Christian Crusaders were on their way to invade Palestine, Hassan-i Sabbah formed the sect made of Iranian Shia Muslims. Its main goal was to fight against Sunni Muslims and Seljuk Turks and murder their leaders throughout the Middle East. Sometimes they even conducted assassinations for Christian rulers of Palestine and Syria.

The signature mark of a Hashshashin attack was killing with a dagger, preferably in a public space such as a market or mosque. The public setting of the assassination ensured that the message of fear would spread immediately. It also illustrated that assassins could strike anywhere and anytime. They always concentrated on a single target and refrained from unnecessary killings of bystanders or the spread of fear through mass murders. The fearsome sect existed for two centuries until Mongols invaded Iran and destroyed their strongholds.

an important part of social decisions in some European and Latin American countries to this day.

Today's global community is changing much faster than medieval Europe, a reality that leaves Islamic societies in a difficult position. No society, including Muslims, can exist in cultural isolation. But Muslims find it very difficult to accept, absorb, and digest many of the cultural changes that are spreading to much of the rest of the world. To loosen the grip on a rigid and highly structured cultural system can endanger the existence of that system. Yet Islam has no choice if its followers are to keep pace with the advancing global community.

According to Islamic law in Saudi Arabia, women have few personal liberties. They fully depend on the will of their father or husband. If married, they cannot conduct personal matters without first seeking approval. Male dominance is absolute in this country today, just as it was during the Prophet's era. Public executions, including beheadings, are common. Religious policy determines appropriate public behavior and establishes punishments for those who fail to display moral behavior in accordance with Islamic beliefs and teachings. This system is extremely rigid, and Muslim fundamentalists fight to preserve the strict religious policies.

North of Saudi Arabia, just beyond Iraq, is Turkey. Muslims in this country constitute 99 percent of the total population. Amazingly, however, Turkey is a secular country in which the separation of church and state is strictly enforced. It has been that way since the 1920s when political leaders introduced radical changes by opening their society to Western principles. Turkey's leaders eagerly accepted some, but not all, aspects of Western culture, including the alphabet, Western clothing, greater freedoms for women, and certain aspects of democracy.

At the time, many Turks were opposed to change, and the government received an unexpected backlash from conservative citizens. In 1923, modern Turkey rose from the ashes of the Ottoman Empire. The country was formed through bloody revolution in the aftermath of World War I, and the Turks were exhausted. In times of violence and struggle, radical changes can be implemented much easier than during an era of peace and prosperity. When a people are struggling, opposition voices are easier to silence. Despite frequent challenges and calls to allow Islam's influence on a political and socioeconomic level, Turkey remained secular. The answer rests in the fact that the Turkish Islamic cultural system, because of the earlier acceptance of some Western ways, had been less rigid than the Saudis' for several generations. Time allowed Turks to find solutions in balancing the relationship between religion and state.

When a group of terrorists hijacked four planes and used them as bombs on September 11, 2001, their identities were unknown at first. Gradually, intelligence agencies gathered information about the attackers. The public soon realized that most members of this terrorist group were Saudi Arabian citizens. Not a single one of them came from Turkey. After the 2003 U.S. invasion of Iraq, foreign volunteers went to Iraq and started filling the ranks of those fighting against the invaders. During the height of the attacks against American forces and Iraqi government troops, the strongest volunteer and financial support came from Saudi Arabia. Captured foreigners justified their actions in the belief that they were engaged in a holy war. They were protecting Islam and Islamic culture in the face of an attack from the West.

Militant Islam is, in the mind of Islamic terrorists, the only solution that can prevent the collapse of their cultural system.

THE PROFILE OF ISLAMIC TERRORISTS

There are numerous groups labeled as terrorist organizations in the Islamic world. Their means are similar, but their goals differ greatly. For example, Hizbollah strives to dominate Lebanon's political sphere and is structured as a political party. Its members run for legitimate positions in the national assembly. The organization provides many social services in areas where it holds a strong position. It is Hizbollah's military branch that engages in widely condemned acts of classic terrorism. Hizbollah's clear goal is to promote the interests of the Lebanese Shia by inserting itself as Lebanon's leading political party.

Among Palestinians, international authorities recognize several terrorist groups because of their attacks on Israel's civilian population. These groups have several goals. One, of course, is to gain political independence from Israel. Another is the complete destruction of Israel as a Jewish state. In the early days of the Israeli–Palestinian conflict, Islam had little success as the driving force behind Palestinian unity. Some Palestinian nationalists in the 1950s and 1960s were not even Muslims, but Christians affiliated with European left-wing groups from which they gathered support.

European universities were well attended by Palestinians. Their culture cherishes learning, and they are among the best-educated people in Southwest Asia. Many left-leaning European intellectuals resented Jewish and Israeli policies and therefore supported pro-Palestinian causes. Palestinians also received military support from the Soviet Union in the form of weapons.

In the last two decades, Palestinian nationalists have accepted a much stronger religious influence, particularly with the rise of the Hamas movement. Hamas was the new generation's response to the Palestinians' failure to create a new country. Decades of rapid population growth in Palestinian refugee camps created thousands of angry young men who saw little prospect for their future. Dissatisfied with leading Palestinian Yasir Arafat and his Fatah party, they wanted immediate changes. This is when Hamas stepped in.

As noted in the previous chapter, young people are filled with energy and want quick and radical solutions. But they often lack leadership and guidance. Hamas, formed in 1987, added a religious element to Palestinian militantism. Hamas's volunteers transformed suicide bombing into a sophisticated exercise of terrorism and received widespread Palestinian acceptance.

Unable to compete with Israel in open warfare, Hamas drastically increased the frequency of terrorist attacks on civil targets deep inside Israel.

Hamas-sponsored bombings lifted the spirits of many desperate Palestinians. They believed that such a response, including civilian deaths, was appropriate against what they believed was Israel's brutality over Palestinians. Hamas also learned from Hizbollah's experience, and by the early 2000s, transformed into one of the leading Palestinian political parties. It engaged in both militant and political activities. Leaders emphasized social services and the building of hospitals and schools. Because most Palestinians suffer from poverty and are socially marginalized, this helped Hamas gain strong support. This is further evidence of the way in which blending church and state can be effective in Islamic societies. Today, Hamas controls the Palestinian social, political, economic, and military sphere in the Gaza area. Much of its success can be attributed to its following of Islamic teachings and ethics.

Hamas and Hizbollah are the most prominent terrorist groups in Southwest Asia. There are others. The foregoing examples, however, provide the reader with some insight into the structure of Islamic terrorism. One additional cultural detail warrants discussion. It is an intriguing indicator of Islamic terrorists' psychology. In the context of this chapter, it may provide an additional glimpse into a major dilemma facing the Islamic cultural system.

Two layers exist in the basic makeup of a terrorist organization, including al Qaeda. At one level are the field operatives and recruiters who interact with potential suicide bombers. Their assignments include the actual completion of an attack planned by another layer involved in strategy planning and decision making. Individuals who actually conduct a suicide bombing are almost always from lower socioeconomic backgrounds. Or, in some cases, their families have suffered in some way at the hands of the perceived oppressor (the target of terrorist bombings). Among Palestinians, that may include a family member who lost a loved one in Israeli artillery's shelling of their neighborhood. In Iraq, terrorists recruit from families similarly affected by American military activity. Revenge is a force powerful enough for one to give up his or her life while taking as many others as possible. Few doctors, lawyers, or other affluent citizens, however, are willing to blow themselves up.

There is also an upper rank of terrorists, those involved in the management of a terrorist organization. These leaders are generally well educated. Many of them are persuasive speakers (often in many languages), well traveled, and holders of university degrees. It is not unusual for them to come from wealthy families. Their ability to convey a message to a global audience is highly valued. After all, terrorists want their message to spread as rapidly and to as large an audience as possible. It is their background that reveals some interesting cultural details and perhaps explains why affluent, well-educated people join terrorist networks.

A surprisingly large number of well-educated Islamic terrorists come from the physical science, medical, or engineering field. This reflects their individual preference. But it also reflects a strong Arab world cultural preference: By a wide margin, they prefer "hard" sciences over the more controversial social sciences. Cultural geographers, anthropologists, philosophers, and sociologists simply are not found among the ranks of Islamic terrorists.

The situation within the Arab world is exactly the opposite of left-wing terrorists elsewhere. In Europe and North America, nearly all of the radical leftists during the 1950s and 1960s were educated in the social sciences. How can this sharp difference in backgrounds be explained? Social scientists study (and often challenge) existing philosophical and human principles. Their ideas are often abstract. For example, they may challenge many religious viewpoints and teachings, including the existence of God or the nature of truth.

As noted earlier, the traditional cultural beliefs that are integrated into Islam are held sacred. They cannot be challenged.

Any criticism of Islamic doctrine is considered a challenge (and an insult) to Islam itself. Physical sciences deal with scientific reality, whereas social scientists challenge existing social theory. Social sciences are simply not widely accepted in Islamic society. There can be no challenges to Islam, or to the authoritarian governments that tend to dominate the Islamic world.

Furthermore, social scientists study and attempt to understand other cultures. They tend to be quite liberal in accepting cultural differences (including other religions). It is not surprising that the main ideas of the eighteenth-century European Enlightenment were formulated by people with social science backgrounds. In the United States, Thomas Jefferson and other Founding Fathers relied on the ideas of European philosophers while drafting the Declaration of Independence.

For whatever reason, Arab culture continues to turn its back on the social sciences. If the Arab-Muslim world hopes to take its place within today's closely linked global community, it must understand and be tolerant of others, including those of different religious beliefs. There are few signs, however, that this is happening.

Physical scientists (such as biologists and physicists) develop and test hypotheses and formulate laws. They begin with an idea and, if it works, there is a satisfactory conclusion. Engineers design things, such as tunnels or bridges. Both work using a process that has a beginning and an end. For physical scientists and engineers, the objects of their interest and professional work are largely *objective*. In social sciences and philosophy, on the other hand, there are few laws and many questions remain open-ended. They are far more *subjective* in nature. The existence of God, for example, cannot be proven scientifically. One accepts or rejects the idea on the basis of feelings and faith.

In the Islamic system, then, the strongest advocates of terrorism are individuals least practiced to intellectually discuss abstract cultural issues, or accept the social views of others. Knowing this, one can better understand the source of their extreme frustration. Due to their lack of understanding, they fear new "Western" ideas. Certainly this is not to say that all physical scientists, engineers, or medical doctors in Muslim countries are going to be terrorists! There is clear evidence, however, of the relationship between educational background and participation in Muslim terrorist organizations.

AL QAEDA

In late 1979, the Soviet Union invaded Afghanistan. Its goal was to effectively support Afghanistan's Communists. Since the end of World War II, the Soviets feared that neighboring countries might engage them in another German-like invasion. They actively worked to form a protective "buffer zone" around their enormous homeland. After the invasion, fighting in Afghanistan increased in intensity. It became clear that a peaceful solution was out of reach. Stern opposition to the Soviet presence and the Afghani government turned into widespread guerrilla warfare. The guerrillas were known as *mujahideen*. They received support from Pakistan and the United States. Both countries sought to prevent further southward expansion of the Soviet Union's buffer zone. Volunteers from other Muslim countries, mainly Arab nations, flocked to Afghanistan. Thousands of them joined the anti-Communist resistance against what they thought was an attack on Islam itself. Among them was a Saudi Arabian, Osama bin Laden.

During his years in Afghanistan, bin Laden met many foreign fighters and established connections with like-minded individuals. There was a widely held belief that Islam was under assault from the West. It provided fuel for the growing idea that a vast Muslim-ruled empire must be created. The boundaries of this new nation would resemble those of the medieval Arab empire that once stretched from China to the Atlantic Ocean. Many Muslim extremists supported this idea. After the Soviet Union fell apart in 1991, their attention immediately turned to the power

Afghan guerrillas pose with an unexploded Soviet bomb in the mountains near Pakistan's border in 1981. The United States funded these *mujahideen* in an effort to limit Soviet expansion, but these same rebels produced America's greatest enemy, Osama bin Laden.

they saw as being the primary sponsor of conflict in Afghanistan: the United States.

The American presence in the Gulf region, particularly in Saudi Arabia, additionally fueled the sentiments of militants. Osama bin Laden came from a wealthy and influential Saudi Arabian family. His personal fortune amounted to hundreds of millions of dollars. He used his fortune to create a terrorist body that would become known as al Qaeda.

By the end of the 1990s, several major attacks were planned and executed around the world, mainly against American military and civilian targets. In 1993, the first bombing of New York City's World Trade Center occurred when a truck bomb exploded in one of the towers' garages. Two years later, a plan to hijack eleven civilian aircraft was foiled by alert Philippine authorities. In 1998, simultaneous explosions destroyed American embassies in Nairobi, Kenya, and Dar es Salaam, Tanzania. With this event,

MAKING CONNECTIONS

In an age of unprecedented growth of electronic communication, news travels fast. But news from many countries is tailored to fit various political beliefs and agendas. In the Islamic world, it has become increasingly customary for masses to irrationally react to news with violence. This is true of deeds or events that occur in distant lands. In Pakistan, for example, thousands of people may take to the streets over something that occurs in faraway Europe or Africa. In the West, incorrect reporting by journalists affects our point of view. Information in articles we read may suffer from poor translation of a foreign leader's statements. Or it may be nothing more than propaganda. Actions on both sides contribute to an overall increase in violence throughout the world. What responsibilities do local and worldwide media have to tell the truth fairly and impartially? Do you believe that a country has the right to bend the truth in the media if it is for its own good? What would be your solution to these problems?

it became obvious that bin Laden's terrorist organization had vastly expanded goals and growing support. The September 11, 2001, attacks in the United States gave ample proof of the extent of their operation. Al Qaeda also was responsible for deadly attacks on Americans and their allies in Saudi Arabia and other Gulf countries. Its affiliates planned and executed a number of bombings from Europe to Indonesia.

Al Qaeda's major success has been its ability to create an organization with a loose hierarchical structure while developing global connections. But the brutality and geographical distribution of attacks, together with the high number of civilian casualties, magnify the actual capability of this network. Even when its connections with local extremists are loose, the media tends to portray attacks as the al Qaeda mastermind's latest challenge to global peace.

Media coverage of global terrorism creates an image of powerful terrorist forces working closely together to achieve their goals. This simply is not true. Elaborate security measures were put in place in the United States after the 2001 tragedy. Since that time, as of the publication of this book, no further major incidents have occurred in the United States. Despite many objections by a public concerned about violations to its constitutional rights, the government's security measures have worked. This is quite amazing, considering the country's huge area and population, its population's easy access to firearms, its focus on individual freedoms, and its rather porous land borders. In addition, some of the leading figures in al Qaeda have been killed or captured, including Khalid Sheikh Mohammad, the planner of the September 11 attacks. Despite enduring several devastating bombings, Europeans also have been able to generally contain terror activity on their soil. Compared to a decade ago, al Qaeda's ability to freely strike almost anywhere in the world has been drastically reduced.

6

SECURITY

It is impossible to prevent all terrorist attacks. As terrorists aim to spread fear and destruction, while keeping their human and material losses at a minimum, they rely on ingenuity as their most precious weapon. The forces battling terrorism must always remain a step ahead in order to provide adequate security. This is rather difficult to achieve even with the most sophisticated equipment and intelligence available. Terrorists learn from past mistakes and adjust their approach. The assassination of public officials may prove to be difficult because of tight security. But a lit cigarette thrown in a forest can successfully ignite a fire that can result in billions of dollars in damage. Oil pipelines can be sabotaged in Iraq, Nigeria, or elsewhere. It requires only access and a small amount of explosives. Yet damage to a pipeline can create havoc on the commodity exchange market and can affect the global economy in a variety of negative ways. This chapter describes some common approaches in the global prevention of terrorism and lists security responses.

LAW ENFORCEMENT

International and domestic terrorism can be reduced with appropriate law enforcement. Most countries have antiterrorism bodies created through legislative measures. Terrorists may operate on a local or regional level. But they often interact with like-minded individuals and organizations through a global network of associates and communication linkages. The age when political boundaries served as significant physical and communication barriers to terrorists is over. Communication, technology, and finances continuously slip through international channels. This is why preventive law-enforcement policies and measures must be in place.

Countries increasingly share their experiences with one another directly and through international law enforcement bodies such as Interpol. Short for International Criminal Police Organization, this agency was created in 1923 to increase cooperation among national police agencies. Today it is active in nearly all nations. Its database contains names of common criminals on the run and also people wanted for their terrorism-related activities. On a number of occasions, al Qaeda affiliates were detained after being identified at border crossings and airports with the help of Interpol's database. Before the age of computers, data exchange was slow, but recent improvements have been impressive. This is particularly significant in database research for suspects' fingerprints and DNA samples. What previously took weeks and months is now available in a matter of hours.

Terrorists often count on common criminals for fund-raising. In Afghanistan, for example, al Qaeda and fundamentalist Islamic militia the Taliban oversee production of opium and heroin. They then harvest profits and use the funds to purchase military hardware or to finance supporters. These narcotics are manufactured from poppy seeds grown by peasant farmers throughout Afghanistan. The country is the world's leading producer of opium and heroin. Farmers plant and harvest their crop, but someone needs to manufacture it into drugs and transport it to consumers worldwide. This is when regular outlaws—Afghan "warlords"—step in and do their part of the business cycle. From Afghanistan through Iran and the former Soviet Republic, drugs are shipped westward. A network of associates makes sure that the shipment eventually reaches the market. The Taliban oversees trafficking by not interrupting it, for which they receive their own portion of the profits, which may arrive in the form of money, arms, or other necessary types of supplies.

Even though it is against their religious beliefs to do such things, the Taliban learned that drug trafficking is a lucrative business and an excellent form of fund-raising. Afghanistan is a country in disarray. Law-enforcement activities do not extend outside of the capital, Kabul, and other major cities. International

BIOMETRICS

With continuous technological advancement, terrorism-prevention measures have expanded into what was previously assumed to be the domain of science fiction. Biometrics is the measurement and statistical study of human physical features. This information can be used to identify physical differences among humans. DNA analysis, electronic fingerprinting, comparison of facial uniqueness, retina identification, and voice recognition are some of the main aspects of biometric-related security applications.

In order to limit terrorist infiltration, law enforcement in many countries depends on biometric databases. Passport-producing technology is becoming increasingly sophisticated with the ability to include more and more biometric data. Proponents of biometrics as an antiterrorist and security tool in general welcome such technological ability. Critics, on the other hand, fear that biometrics represent yet another step toward the complete loss of personal liberties and the creation of a "big brother" civilization.

military forces present in Afghanistan are occupied with daily engagements and protection of urban areas. Poppy seeds are grown in a lawless countryside in a country the size of Texas, and it is currently impossible to oversee such a vast area. This is where international cooperation steps in through the exchange of information and data sharing. Each time a shipment is intercepted in Russia, Turkey, or elsewhere, supply channels to Afghani terrorists are cut off.

The international narcotics trade in Latin America works in a similar way, through the distribution of cocaine to finance rebels hiding in the countryside. Colombian drug cartels are not necessarily involved in political affairs. But they certainly don't mind the money they receive for transporting cocaine for FARC to the United States.

THE TRAIL OF MONEY

Terrorist activity is expensive, and obtaining funds is essential to any operation. In a war-torn country like Iraq, it is quite easy for terrorists to find support. It is much more difficult under normal conditions, however, because money always leaves behind a trail. Law-enforcement and intelligence agencies constantly search for such trails. In fact, tracking terrorists' finances is one of the best tools available for the prevention of terrorist infiltration and attack. Unfortunately, these agencies also have to learn from their own mistakes, often after deadly attacks already have happened.

Following the devastating attacks of September 11, 2001, it became clear that al Qaeda operatives could not have conducted the attack without using an elaborate financial scheme. Their U.S. accounts were funded with transactions from overseas banks in order to pay for various expenses, including tuition for flight training. Credit card transactions left a trail that provided the FBI with information about their movements. Internet purchases also could be traced back to a specific computer.

The system for preventing international money laundering and terrorism financing already existed prior to September 11. United States federal law prohibits transport of larger volumes of undeclared cash. All excessive sums must be reported to U.S. Customs agents when entering the country. To finance its operation, al Qaeda had to transfer substantial sums electronically to bank accounts in the United States. This way, terrorists did not risk arrest by passing through airport customs with huge sums of money. That would have put their plan in danger. Once financial accounts like these are open, they can be easily accessed. But they also, with a court order, can be monitored by the FBI.

Since 2001, the United States and some European countries have drastically increased the quality of control over terrorists' financial dealings. That alone assisted in breaking several terrorist cells. At the same time, these nations acquired substantial knowledge about the inner workings of terrorist groups. The ability to interrupt the flow of money proved to be a very valuable tool in the fight against terrorism. A number of individuals were detained and prosecuted on grounds of funding terrorists in the Middle East based on the money trail. Contributions to some Islamic charities were being diverted to terrorist coffers. Charities, many of which are associated with religious institutions, can be infiltrated by the terrorists. They can then siphon off the organizations' finances for their own benefit.

Following the money trail is also a valuable way to prevent state-sponsored terrorism. Purchase of military hardware can be tracked through international financial channels. In this way, financing of covert operations can be publicly exposed. Iraq's chemical attack on Kurds, for example, occurred after the government purchased large quantities of chemicals on the global market.

Even the United States is not immune to clandestine activities. During the infamous Iran–Contra affair of 1986,

Afghanistan's opium poppy fields make the country the leading source of heroin in the world. This big business funds the terrorist activities of the Taliban and al Qaeda.

investigators determined that high-ranking White House officials were involved in illegal arms trade. Again, a money trail provided the primary clue. The complex scheme included the United States, Israel, and Iran. Basically, a deal was made to provide Iran with missiles in exchange for Hizbollah's release of hostages in Lebanon. The money received from the Iranian purchase was diverted to finance antigovernment and anti-Communist guerrillas, or the Contras, in the Nicaraguan civil war. Additional funding for the Contras was obtained, among other ways, through insurance fraud.

COMMUNICATION INTERCEPTION

One vital advantage in the global war on terrorism is the ability of antiterrorist units to intercept communications without terrorists' knowledge. This allows authorities to know in advance about potential attacks and to take appropriate countermeasures. The fight against terrorism is very complex. Interception of communications is an essential security strategy in the battle against terrorism.

The global communication network, however, is huge and impossible to monitor everyplace, all of the time. Terrorists, of course, learn quickly from their mistakes. They continuously develop new ways of communicating in order to avoid detection. Intelligence agencies closely monitor telephone communication and Internet traffic, particularly e-mail exchanges and conversations in chat rooms. In most instances, messages are hidden and experts must decode them without revealing their activities.

Communication interception is not exactly what we see in Hollywood's conspiracy-theory productions. But various governments do, indeed, closely monitor global communication networks. U.S. military and intelligence agencies spend billions of dollars annually just to eavesdrop on communication networks around the world. Information that passes through commercial satellites, fiber-optic cables, and the Internet is monitored and accessed if necessary. In fact, many governments have legal rights to spy on their own citizens to combat terrorism as outlined in their constitutions. In the United States, especially after 2001, snooping into private conversations conducted by American citizens has been a matter of serious public debate. Supporters of this program argue that protecting human lives is not interference in private affairs and personal freedoms. The opposing side questions the constitutionality of measures that allow the release of individuals' private information without probable cause. Of particular concern was the release of data by the leading cellular-phone operators to U.S. intelligence agencies.

A good example of how control over communication can produce important results is the 1996 assassination of Chechen rebel leader Dzhokhar Dudayev. During the turbulent years in Russia following the downfall of the Soviet Union in 1991, the autonomous republic of Chechnya proclaimed independence. Chechen troops engaged in open warfare against Russian forces. As a former Soviet military officer, Dudayev was a skilled soldier able to evade Russian troops for years. His units inflicted many serious military blows with guerrilla and terrorist-style attacks. Despite superior military power, the Russians failed to crush Chechen resistance and eliminate Dudayev. Finally, in 1996, the Russian military was in a position to intercept one of Dudayev's conversations conducted over satellite telephone. This was enough to indicate his location in a Chechen village. Soon after, it was confirmed that the person on the phone was indeed Dudayev. An aircraft delivered a missile into the hideout, instantly killing the Chechen leader. Thousands of troops on the ground were unable to produce results that were finally accomplished after the interception of a single phone conversation.

RECONNAISSANCE AND SURVEILLANCE

Interception of communication is only one aspect of antiterrorist security. A variety of reconnaissance and surveillance options are available to security forces. Advanced technology has made military hardware increasingly sophisticated. Instead of counting on manpower, many countries use satellites, unmanned aerial vehicles (UAV), and unmanned aircraft for assignments previously unimaginable. They transport real-time data to command centers, where it can be processed in a short period of time, leaving enough time for decision making.

Because of their delicate security situation, Israelis are among the leaders in reconnaissance and surveillance. Israel is a small country surrounded by countries where anti-Jewish sentiments run high. To protect its territory and scattered Jewish settlements from Palestinian gunmen's rocket attacks, Israel conducts continuous air surveillance of the region. Palestinian rockets are fired from urban areas. When Israeli forces retaliate, there is great concern over causing civilian casualties. In the past, Israel often was condemned by the international community for responding to attacks by shelling the centers of Palestinian cities in pursuit of targets. This kind of publicity works well for anti-Israeli propaganda. On the other hand, the increasing number of civilian casualties on Israel's side has led to demands for stern preventive actions.

Faced with a no-win situation, Israelis realized that a rapid and accurate response was the best option. They developed new methods of surveillance of Palestinian- and Hizbollah-controlled areas. Unmanned aircraft equipped with television cameras and missiles are now capable of striking anywhere, but with previously unmatched precision. Specially designed ammunition reaches the target and explodes in a small radius, which drastically reduces civilian casualties. Israel's response previously included artillery or fighter jet shelling that created vast damage and loss of life. By the time fighter planes arrived, militants already were gone, as they had enough time to retreat to their urban hideouts. An unmanned aircraft can fly overhead for many hours. It also can fire at a target on a moment's notice from a remotely controlled signal.

Unmanned aerial vehicles (UAV), including unmanned aircraft, proved valuable in other counterterrorism operations as well. In Iraq and Afghanistan, they cover large geographical areas in pursuit of insurgents. A live image provides detailed information about their movement, numbers, and military strength. The U.S. military currently uses several different unmanned aerial vehicles and aircraft, most notably Predator, Reaper, and Global Hawk. Equipped with Hellfire missiles, they can reach stationary and moving targets and at the same time survey thousands of square miles of land. In some countries, such as Pakistan, overt American military intervention is out of the question. When terrorists slip back across the porous border with Afghanistan, their shelters can be targeted by UAVs.

The UAVs' major success outside of the battlefields occurred in 2002 in Yemen. After pursing the planners of the attack on the USS *Cole* in Aden a few years earlier, a Hellfire missile

Out of necessity, Israeli reconnaissance and surveillance technology is the world's most advanced. This 2007 photo shows the new Heron unmanned drone aircraft, a valuable weapon in counterterrorism.

launched from Predator killed six al Qaeda operatives, including the attack's planner. A similar attack on the ground would have had to include the Special Forces teams. They would have had to penetrate the hostile environment of Yemen's tribal areas and undoubtedly experience many casualties.

Closed-circuit television (CCTV) is the ground equivalent of air surveillance vehicles. In the past, CCTV was used mainly to deter criminals from breaking and entering. The technology is now an integral part of antiterrorism efforts around the world. Cameras installed on buildings and streetlight poles survey a specific area and transmit the signal for storage and processing. This surveillance option is particularly popular in the United Kingdom. CCTV video records helped identify the al Qaeda bombers of the London Underground in 2005. As this system is used mainly by police, privacy issues are now a part of public debate.

TRAINING AND INFILTRATION

All technological advances aside, old-fashioned methods are still a reliable way of penetrating terrorist networks and cells. It is very difficult, however, to infiltrate such organizations with agents and informants. Secrecy and brutality are two main characteristics in the cultural system of terrorism. Few people are willing to volunteer for that kind of undercover assignment. If their true identity is revealed, agents are usually tortured and killed. The lucky ones survive to be pawns in a prisoner swap.

Yet when such assignments are successful, the benefits are great. Psychologically, terrorists fear few things more than the realization that one of them could be an informant. Operationally, all bets are off and the network must be built from the ground up again to avoid detection. In 2008, when Colombian forces rescued hostages held by FARC for many years, a serious blow was dealt to this terrorist organization. It was announced that information leading to the successful rescue mission came from government agents who had infiltrated FARC's ranks.

It takes time and patience to infiltrate a tight network. Some groups are more likely than others to lose control over their internal security, depending upon their overall structure and mission. For example, the FBI is better able to plant an agent among right-wing hate groups than the CIA is among Afghani villagers. Skinheads or the Klan welcome new members from the outside in order to increase numbers. An unfamiliar cultural environment, however, creates additional challenges. Tight tribal structures and relationships based on blood lineages are the best defense against the outside force. Newcomers are always under suspicion, and identifying sympathizers who would help infiltration is a hard task. Despite greedy Afghani warlords and high monetary rewards offered for bin Laden, the

MAKING CONNECTIONS

Is an attack on an independent country, even if it is done as a preventive measure against terrorism, a wise long-term security choice for the global community? Or does such an action only allow additional excuses for powerful countries to overthrow governments of weak countries, even where no provable terrorist ties exist? How would you approach this sensitive issue if you were in a situation where you had to make decisions affecting future world geopolitics?

protectors of al Qaeda's leadership have prevented his arrest all these years.

Realizing that cultural barriers create serious obstacles in the global war on terrorism, the United States' military and intelligence decided to employ a different approach. Instead of independently conducting risky and what could be characterized as illegal assignments in other countries, advisers were sent to educate and train local forces in combating terrorism. American forces are present in more than 100 countries today. They are cooperating with host nations to counter terrorism. In the southern Philippines, for example, American advisers have trained local security forces in intelligence-gathering techniques. Philippine forces are able to conduct their own security operations. As a result of this cooperative effort, an al Qaeda–affiliated terrorist group, Abu Sayyaf, has been contained and its ranks have been decimated.

In combating global terrorism, the most important aspect of infiltration and training is to gain the sympathy of the local civilian population. Community leaders sometimes can be bought, bribed, or pressured in some other way to change sides. But if the entire community's sentiment is inclined toward terrorists (as in the Afghanistan/Pakistan borderlands), then most efforts are fruitless.

In Catholic parts of Belfast, Ireland, as noted earlier, a majority of residents initially supported separatist tendencies by the Irish Republican Army. This created a serious barrier for the British security forces to penetrate, while allowing the IRA to enjoy a safe haven among Belfast's Catholics. Once the IRA's attacks shifted from military to civilian targets, much of its popular support withered away. British intelligence discovered more individuals willing to cooperate. In Iraq, al Qaeda fanned flames of conflict throughout entire cities. Only then did local tribesmen, with U.S. materials and financial help, finally organize into Awakening Councils and begin to drive most terrorists away.

7

THE FUTURE OF TERRORISM

Terrorism cannot be extinguished like a fire. Solving social and cultural issues in an aggressive, rather than a peaceful, way has been a crucial part of our lifestyle since prehistoric times. Desire for power and the fight against the powerful, both by violent means, were not exceptions to the rule. They were the rule. But in our cultural evolution, humans managed to improve living conditions, and through institutional development, we've opened doors to dialogue. Never before in history have humans experienced less violence than we do today.

Given the historical role of conflict, it takes time to digest the idea that finding non-violent solutions to difficult problems is essential if humans are to live in harmony. During the first half of the twentieth century, it was unimaginable that Europe would one day rise from the ashes of two world wars and become peaceful and united. Patience and power-sharing have never been strong human virtues. Frustration and despair behind impatience are too frequently the main driving forces for contemporary terrorism. With patience, though, we are able to conquer many obstacles and create long-term prosperity.

A look at twentieth-century history is all that is needed in order to see the long list of unnecessary conflicts that could have been avoided by thoughtful dialogue. World War I began when royal cousins from Germany, Russia, and the United Kingdom decided to show off their prestige to one another. It eventually cost Europe tens of millions of lives. Impatience in political dialogue created a slaughterhouse throughout the early 1990s in the former Yugoslavia and Rwanda. When they look back to times of genocide and widespread terror, people in these countries, or in what is left of them, ask themselves a single question: Did we need this? Neither the Israeli nor the Palestinian side would propose continuing to live in constant fear from terrorism instead of enjoying peace and prosperity. Yet for many generations, terrorism has been a daily occurrence in their part of the world.

In the motion picture *The Man Who Would Be King*, made after Rudyard Kipling's story, two opportunistic English soldiers of fortune (played by Sean Connery and Michael Caine) arrive in Kafiristan to conquer the region and become kings. (Kafiristan is the remote mountainous region in present-day Pakistan and perhaps one of the current hideouts for Osama bin Laden.) The story takes place at the beginning of the twentieth century. After arriving in a village and liberating it from the neighboring tribe's attacks, the Englishmen are introduced to the village chief. Grateful for liberation, but scared of the men who he thought were gods, the chief listens to the Englishmen's proposition translated by a Gurkha soldier:

> "Tell him that Baskhai could be only the beginning. That we hopes [sic] to go on from victory to victory until he runs out of enemies."
>
> "Monarch of all he surveys."
>
> When this was conveyed to him, Ootah stared open-mouthed, almost as if entranced.

> "*All* he surveys?" Billy Fish asked for him.
> "From the highest place in this valley..."
> "The mountains will echo his name..."
> "Ootah the Great."
> The headman spoke sharply at this.
> "Preferring Ootah the Terrible."
> Carnehan made his little bow again.
> "Ootah the Terrible it shall be."

From there, the two proceed with the conquest of other villages and eventually the entire region of Kafiristan, with greedy Ootah's head being cut off along the way. Each time they conquer a new village, they order that ongoing feuds with enemies end immediately. In a short period of time, Kafiristan becomes an oasis of peace for the first time ever. And the Englishmen do indeed scam their way to becoming the leaders of Kafiristan, as one of them is assumed to be a god.

Soon after, they implement the rule of law, begin presiding over feuds between peasants, and introduce the expansion of infrastructure for the common good. Bridges connect previously impassable gorges. The idea of "civilizing" Kafiristan suddenly becomes an issue more important than simply stealing its gold and rubies. The life of the local people becomes better than before. They are forced to share during times of need, instead of stealing, and to help each other instead of pillaging neighboring villages. In this process, the Englishmen show little respect to the local folk traditions and religious beliefs as they consider them primitive and useless.

Their adventure ends after the Englishmen are revealed as not being gods, but men. In a symbolic scene, the soldier played by Sean Connery is forced to walk to the middle of a freshly constructed bridge. The ropes are then cut, and the "god" Englishman falls into the abyss. Kafiristanis then return back to their previous way of life in disarray and feud.

A cloaked woman appears in the town center of Sanaa, Yemen. Until people can agree to respect ideologies and cultures different from their own, fear and desperation are likely to continue the threat of terrorism around the world.

Although brief and rather general, this movie synopsis reminds us about the extent of contemporary terrorism that is conducted as the result of cultural misunderstanding. The theme of this book and this series is global connections. It means that no portion of the globe can remain isolated for long. In fact, it would be difficult to find a place on Earth that, in the following couple of decades, will not fully embrace globalization. But in this process, the adjustment cannot occur overnight. People cannot replace their cultural beliefs with a flip of the switch. This is particularly important to those who feel they have to change the core of their culture in order to survive. Just like the Kafiris, many other groups prefer the way of life they have practiced for millennia. They feel threatened by those changes that will bring many new and strange traits that have the potential to shake the very foundation of their culture's existence.

Religion and the sense of ethnic belonging are the two most important cultural traits that people feel are being lost on the path to globalization. It is entirely normal that in many countries people fear change. The prospect of becoming a powerless minority can trigger a strong cultural survival instinct and a violent response. The coming decades almost certainly will experience an increase in turbulence, particularly in multicultural countries

THE DISENFRANCHISED

The most bizarre terrorist events sometimes have little to do with ideology, religion, or wars. Acts of angry individuals who seek historic remembrance for the deliberate spread of death and fear are on the increase. To make things worse, copycat killings are not unusual. High schools, universities, churches, shopping malls, and other previously safe havens are now targets. With seemingly increasing frequency, antisocial and emotionally distressed persons are performing violent acts.

Bulletproof security measures are impossible to implement in such cases, because suspects are too difficult to identify in advance. Their often reclusive lifestyles and lack of social interaction drastically limits the possibility for prevention against the deadly assaults. For example, it took many years and a stroke of luck to identify the "Unabomber," Ted Kaczynski. He was a notorious terrorist who devised bombs in a remote cabin in the mountains of Montana. From there he mailed sixteen bombs to chosen targets across the country, killing three and injuring 23.

Despite one of the largest pursuits in FBI history, the leads remained fruitless. It was Kaczynski's brother who finally realized that his sibling was the Unabomber and reported him to the authorities.

in the less-developed world. There, many burning ethnic issues remain unresolved.

Unless we return to a highly polarized world, as was the case during the Cold War, it is highly unlikely that the planet will become a victim of massive global terrorism. Not even the decades-long confrontation between the United States and the Soviet Union was able to fully create such conditions. Today, there is a widespread fear that militant Islam could become a global polarizing force. Despite the current spotlight on Southwest Asia and the Muslim world in general, it is very doubtful that this will occur.

In the West, terrorism is drifting into several new directions. For example, the current concern held by many over potential global warming and other environmental issues is stirring passions. Instead of reading Chairman Mao's ideas, as their parents did, the latest generation of Western radicals is increasingly concentrating on *the planet in peril*. Ecoterrorism is on the rise, not in death tolls, but certainly in terms of material damage and media coverage.

What does the future hold for state-sponsored terrorism during the coming decades? The traditional practice of spreading fear through blatant disregard for the global community's opinion, and its signed international agreements, may vanish. As the global community becomes increasingly connected, rogue states and their leaders will find it increasingly difficult to spread terror.

Today, many countries possess awesome military power. Some, of course, possess nuclear weapons and other weapons of mass destruction. But some hard lessons may have been learned during the bitter conflicts of the twentieth century. On many occasions during World War I and World War II, more lives were lost in a single day than have been lost during the total period of U.S. military involvement in the Middle East.

We continue to disagree, and in some instances, come to blows. Although the destruction is often devastating, it cannot match that of the atomic bombs used to end Japan's role in World War II. In the past, the primary tactical goal of warfare was loss of lives and destruction of property. Today, the strategy is more apt to be psychological. The New York City public transit authority posts a message, "If you see something, say something." We are being conditioned to jump to perilous conclusions in the name of our own safety. "That young girl standing next to me; it is warm, why is she wearing a heavy coat? Could she be . . . ?" A rather terrifying thought, isn't it! This is what the terrorists are trying to achieve—doubt, fear, and distrust. Where and when will terrorism strike next? Who will be responsible? Who will suffer its consequences? As you have seen in the pages of this book, terrorism is extremely complex. And today's terrorism is by no means local in nature; its tentacles reach worldwide.

GLOSSARY

counterterrorism Active measures designed to inflict losses to terrorist organizations and lead to their eventual elimination.

coup d'état Overthrow of an existing government, often by violent means, by a small group of conspirators.

despot Ruler with absolute power.

developing world Previously referred to as the "Third World" and "less developed world"; countries that are in various stages of the process of industrialization.

ethnic(ity) Term usually used in reference to various groups when a population is culturally diverse.

faction A group of people, usually part of a political organization, who share the same belief.

FARC Revolutionary Armed Forces of Colombia; leftist organization labeled as a terrorist by a number of countries, including the United States.

folk culture Traditional way of life in socially cohesive and rural preindustrial society; the opposite of popular culture.

fundamentalism The practice of reducing a religion to its fundamental core, particularly by interpreting its sacred texts in a literal way.

geopolitics Countries' political and military behavior and decisions in international relations on the basis of global or regional physical and/or human geography.

guerrilla Member of a small military group that uses tactics such as sabotage and harassment to fight a larger, more established military or government.

ideology Ideas or beliefs.

imperialism Policy of extending rule over another state.

infidel A nonbeliever in a certain religion.

junta A small group of people who take over a government, often by violent means.

left-wing The side of the political spectrum that ranges from social democracy to Communism and anarchism as extreme forms; advocates collectivism, workers' rights, and welfare state as national socioeconomic principles.

propaganda Information that is spread to promote a cause.

puppet state Government that is appointed and directed by another government.

race Biological inheritance (as opposed to culture, or learned behavior).

radicals Those seeking revolutionary change in government.

right-wing The side of the political spectrum that ranges from conservative and nationalistic to Fascism as an extreme form; advocates individualism and free enterprise, but also preservation of national wealth in hands of the elite few depending on how far right the socioeconomic principles are.

rogue state A state or nation that acts outside of the accepted international policies, posing a threat of world peace.

secular Not concerned with religion.

terrorism Spread of fear through violence and destruction.

totalitarian System of government in which the state holds all power.

warmonger Person who advocates war.

BIBLIOGRAPHY

Anderson, Sean Kendall, and Stephen Sloan. *Terrorism: Assassins to Zealots*. Lanham, MD: Scarecrow Press, 2002.

Hoffman, Bruce. *Inside Terrorism*. New York, NY: Columbia University Press, 2006.

Pillar, Paul R. *Terrorism and U.S. Foreign Policy*. Washington, DC: The Brookings Institution Press, 2001.

Richardson, Louise, ed. *The Roots of Terrorism*. New York, NY: Routledge, 2006.

White, Leslie A. *The Concept of Cultural Systems: A Key to Understanding Tribes and Nations*. New York, NY: Columbia University Press, 1975.

FURTHER RESOURCES

Badey, Thomas J. *Violence and Terrorism 08/09*. Dubuque, IA: McGraw-Hill, 2008.

Davenport, John C., ed. *Global Extremism and Terrorism*. New York, NY: Chelsea House, 2007.

Gordon, Matthew S. *Islam*. New York, NY: Chelsea House, 2009.

Henderson, Harry. *Global Terrorism*. New York, NY: Facts On File, 2004.

Howard, Russell D., and James J. F. Forest. *Weapons of Mass Destruction and Terrorism*. Dubuque, IA: McGraw-Hill, 2007.

Howard, Russell D., and Reid L. Sawyer. *Terrorism and Counterterrorism: Understanding the New Security Environment, Readings and Interpretations*. Dubuque, IA: McGraw-Hill, 2002.

Moghadam, Assaf. *The Roots of Terrorism*. New York, NY: Chelsea House, 2006.

PICTURE CREDITS

Page

13: © Courtesy of the Library of Congress / LC-USZ62-134452

24: Bradley Brooks / AP Images

30: Martin Cleaver / AP Images

35: © Georges Bartoli / Reuters / Landov

43: AP Images

48: Manish Swarup/ AP Images

56: Dan Staudacher / AP Images

64: © Reuters / Landov

72: © Peter Andrews / Reuters/ Landov

84: Silvano Nencini / AP Images

92: AP Images

96: Ariel Schalit / AP Images

103: © Imagebroker.net / Photolibrary

INDEX

U

V

W

Y

Z

ABOUT THE AUTHOR

ZORAN PAVLOVIĆ is a professional geographer and regular contributor to several Chelsea House series. His books include *Europe* for Modern World Cultures and more than a half dozen titles for the Modern World Nations series. Pavlović's study of terrorism and its consequences is not only based on an extensive background in cultural geography, political science, and history: As a young man in Croatia, he experienced it firsthand during the very turbulent times of the 1990s in the former Yugoslavia.

ABOUT THE EDITOR

CHARLES F. GRITZNER is Distinguished Professor of Geography at South Dakota State University in Brookings. He began college teaching and conducting geographic research in 1960. In addition to teaching, he enjoys travel, writing, working with teachers, and sharing his love of geography with readers. As a senior consulting editor and frequent author for Chelsea House Publishers' Modern World Nations, Major World Cultures, Extreme Environments, and Global Connections series, he has a wonderful opportunity to combine each of these "hobbies." Dr. Gritzner has served as both president and executive director of the National Council for Geographic Education and has received the council's highest honor, the George J. Miller Award for Distinguished Service to Geographic Education, as well as other honors from the NCGE, Association of American Geographers, and other organizations.

